MW01538389

BROKEN PEARL

When Forgiveness Breaks You

F A I T H   T R U A X

ISBN 978-1-0980-1456-8 (paperback)
ISBN 978-1-0980-5058-0 (hardcover)
ISBN 978-1-0980-1457-5 (digital)

Christian Faith Publishing, Inc.
832 Park Avenue
Meadville, PA 16335
www.christianfaithpublishing.com

Scripture quotations are taken from the New King James Version®. Copyright © 1982 by Thomas Nelson, Inc. Used by permission. All rights reserved.

Printed in the United States of America

PREFACE

Sometimes the greatest healing comes from the deepest wounds. Who do you become when a tragedy outweighs your triumphs? When the people you love turn their back on you? And what do you say when you find your greatest love coming from your worst nightmare? Sometimes people love for all the wrong reasons. I chose to love not because I was forced to do it, but I found out that love is a journey, twisting and turning, up and down. When it stops you wish it would go. When it goes, you wish for it to stop. As I sit and write this, I am four months pregnant. I am debating an abortion and my emotional state is somewhat subdued. I have no friends, they are all back home in California. None of them know that I am pregnant. One person, besides my grandmother, who I am living with, knows that I am with child. His name is Chief. Well that's what his friends call him. That's all I knew about him, and the fact that he was just released from jail. I don't remember much from that night except the alcohol on Chief's breath and the short episode I chose to black out of my memory and stash away. But as I look down at my stomach a tear forms in my eye. "What should I do?" "I hate my life. When will this end?" My name is Pearl, and this is my story.

ACKNOWLEDGMENTS

I would first and foremost like to thank my Lord and Savior Jesus Christ. First for his free gift of salvation and also for His never-ending saving grace that at many times has had to catch me when I fall and place me back on my feet. I thank you, Jesus, for never giving up on me, even at times when family, friends, and even myself have given up on me. Thank you for showing me your love, kindness, and understanding at all times of my life. I will never fully understand the many facets of your love for me and all of mankind. Thank you for never giving up on the call you have placed upon my life, even at times when I may have given up.

To my husband Nathan Truax for dealing with all my crap. For hanging in there when I would have left. For balancing all the laundry, bills, and children when I didn't have the "mental" capacity to do it myself. You stuck around when I went through my season of health problems, the doctors' misdiagnosis, my pain and suffering… When I was unable to get out of bed, not able to leave the house, through the psychiatric medication, counseling sessions, and the season when the doctors found the answer. My season of healing and relief, relief from the PTSD, the nervous breakdown, and the hallucinations. You were still there. Though you may not have fully understood it all—and may you never—your unspoken words and actions carried more weight than you could ever imagine. And I will always love you for that. You always have seen God's call on my life, you still see it, and I thank you for always believing in me.

To my two children Kai and Caleb. I love you both more than you could ever imagine. You have taught me so many things, how to love unconditionally, how to have patience, and how to give less of me and all of you. Kai, you were my first baby. I'm sorry for all the mistakes I made as a single mother. My prayer is that you forgive me and find the love I have for you in my heart. You are so special to me and you have taught me what it means to have a mother's love for her children. Caleb, my li'l "Tarzan," I always see your love and joy for life. I pray you never lose that sense of adventure in your heart. I love you so much. I love your "big hugs" in the morning and how you always run to me with a big smile. Kai and Caleb, I love you both so dearly.

Donna Dalton, "DD," thank you for all the love and encouragement you spoke into my life since the first day we met. I don't think a lot of people see the side of you that I've seen. Your love and compassion have never run dry throughout our friendship. You're my secret keeper and truth teller. I've never been afraid to hide who I am when I am with you. I'm not bound to wearing a mask, and for that I thank you! I love and cherish our long talks where there is nothing but laughter and jokes. You were there for me in a very dark time. Our laughter is what pulled me out of that dark place in that moment in time.

My forever friend Lee, you have taught me how to live and love life each day at a time. You will never truly know the impact you have had upon my life. You came at a time when I needed a friend the most. You taught me how to smile and laugh again. You taught me to keep grindin' and to never give up. You are forever a person in my life whom I will always love.

To my pastors, Pastor Jay Haizlip and Christy Haizlip. I thank God for God's call upon your lives, your heart and obedience for His people, and not giving up even at times when I'm sure your road of life got tough. There were so many times in my walk with the Lord that I wanted to give up, I would come to church and the Holy Spirit would radically use you guys to speak into my life to keep going. You will never truly know how much through your obedience God has used you. I dedicate this book to you guys for letting God use you to strengthen my inner woman. I love you guys!

To my mother and father. Thank you for all the sacrifices you guys made for me and Mark. You were caring, amazing, and loving parents in your own way. You always knew how to handle business and take care of your family. You both held on while other marriages were crumbling. I thank you for showing me what love, dedication, and hard work look like. You taught me how to be kind, graceful, and forgiving. To give when it didn't seem possible. To hang on to God always. I will love you always and forever.

For there is hope for a tree.
If it is cut down, that it will sprout again,
And that its tender shoots
Will not cease.
Though its roots may grow
Old in the earth,
And its stump may die in the ground,
Yet at the scent of water it will bud
And bring forth branches like a plant.
(Job 14:7–9)

CHAPTER 1

Five Months Earlier

As I wake up I look at my alarm clock. Ten more minutes until my alarm goes off. I roll over and prop a pillow on top of my head. Darkness fills my vision and I begin to fall into dreamland. I see a picture of my stomach, colors and numbers fill the spaces of darkness. "*Beep, beep, beep!*" I jolt up and look directly into my closet. I smile as I envision what to wear to school. I live in California and love it. My parents own shopping malls throughout Southern California, pretty much making any store in them my personal closet. I own about every bag that you see in all the designer magazines. Any outfit I want, I can have.

Money is no object. I get what I want and at whatever the cost. When I was fifteen years old I wanted lip injections for my birthday, I got it. When I was sixteen I wanted breast implants, I got them. And when I was seventeen I wanted Bradley Cooper to show up at my birthday—well, let's just say I got that also. My parents are alcoholics and know all the who's-who in California. My mother looks like a cat who has had about ten times the legal limit of plastic surgery. My father is a womanizing pig with deep pockets. He cheats on her regularly. But my mother and I don't care. This is our lifestyle and we are comfortable living it. How could anyone else live any different? I could not imagine anything else.

I rummage through my closet looking for my cheerleading uniform. I find it wrapped and hung on a dry-cleaning hanger. I hang it on my doorknob and start to get ready for school. I am sixteen years old, I am a cheerleader for football, and the most popular girl in school. Is it because my parents have a lot of money or is it because I am beautiful? I really don't care as long as I get what I want. I realized at a very young age not to negotiate with people, just manipulate them to get what I want. My boyfriend's name is Trent and we are in love. His dream is to go to law school and to become the president of the United States. I always daydream about living in the White House with him and all the publicity I could get for myself.

I look in the bathroom mirror and realize I have a pimple on my cheek. "Ew, gross." I grab my concealer and dab it on my face. "This should do for now. Wow, I'm gorgeous!" I finish applying my makeup, brush my hair into a ponytail, get dressed, and am out the door. I pass by my mother's room and hear the television blasting. She is passed out with three empty martini glasses next to her bed.

My mother is a wealthy forty-five-year-old woman with too much time on her hands. Her hair, nails, and makeup are always perfect, and she's always shopping and toting our dog Stixx around in some purse carrier. My mother thinks that plastic surgery is just like food, as in everybody needs it to survive. I don't even think that she owns a pair of sweatpants, because I have never even seen her wearing a pair. She is snoring loudly, and the dog is licking her face. My mother still has makeup on her face and is still wearing her day clothes.

I stand beside the bedframe and brush her sandy blonde hair away from her face. Her hair falls next to her oversized chest and pencil thin arms. I can tell by the look of her skin the years are coming up on her and have not been good to her. Behind all that Botox and Restylane there has to be somewhat a good person. All my life my mother has tried to one up me. Although she is ahead of me in her years, somehow she will always try to outdo me. Sometimes I think she hates me or maybe is just jealous of the fact that my father cannot cheat on me personally. It's some sort of sick vendetta. At my sixth birthday party my friends and I decided to perform a dance routine in front of our guests. Well, my mother thought it would be a splendid idea to pop out of a cake and perform an eight count to the Beatles—not once but twice. Not only did she steal my moment, but she also somewhat stole my friends, because after that party half of them did not talk to me anymore.

I run down the stairs, grab my car keys, and jump in my brand-new car my parents bought me for my sweet-sixteen birthday party. I do have to give my parents credit. Whatever I ask them to buy me they buy it. I turn the key to my brand-new Range Rover Sport and rev the engine. The motor purrs while I roll down my windows. The weather is nice and warm, perfect for our homecoming football game tonight. Trent and I are nominated for homecoming king and queen. I reassure myself that we will win tonight. Who else could win? Trent and I are the most popular, richest, and best-looking in our class, why wouldn't we win?

I pull out of the driveway wondering when my mother will awake from her drunken slumber. "Who cares," I think to myself. I blast the music in my car, only to see my father speeding past me and making a mad dash for his parking space. The top is down on his red Ferrari. His shades are covering his tired eyes from another all-nighter with his blonde bimbo Cindy. I wave to him as he smiles at me. "Well hello, my little buttercup!" he yells. He smiles boldly, and from the sparkle in his teeth I can tell he got lucky last night. My father is wearing a light blue sweater and turquoise pants. They match perfectly against his dark hair and dark eyes and tan colored skin. My father is ten years younger than my mom. He is a charming and handsome man. I think his major in school could have been charisma and charm. I turn my music up even more to drown out his annoying voice. His face just wreaks with the stench of his infidelity.

My father has been cheating on my mother for as long as I can remember. When I was about seven years old I remember snooping through his desk, only to find some pictures of him lying on the beach groping some other woman who was not my mom. Every once in a while, I would come across more pictures of my father with various women, all in different places. One picture of him in the Bahamas with a petite brunette clinking champagne glasses over a full roasted pig. Another picture of him standing in front of the Eifel Tower smiling with a beautiful redhead. Dining in China with a slender Asia woman—well, I assumed it was China from the four servants in the picture serving them. After a while I stopped looking for the pictures, but every now and then they would just turn up.

Sometimes I remembered their names, sometimes not. My father would always write the name of each woman on the back of the photo. How classy of him to remember their names, yet disgusting, right?

Usually when he pulls an all-nighter in town he will rush home before my mother wakes up from her drunken slumber. He will usually have our maid Zelda prepare her breakfast, only to tell her that he did it himself. Pretty sneaky, right? I think so, but anything to keep things "cool" between them. My father inherited his fortune from my mother. When my parents met my father was dirt poor, working at a very high-end grocery store bagging my mother's groceries. He was a very attractive young man looking for a way of escape. My mother, being older than him, already divorced, and looking for a young man to "get her groove back," so to speak, locked eyes with my father and the rest is history. Or should I say, "mall history."

After my mother's dad passed away they inherited a huge chunk of change, and my father, being the money-hungry pig that he is, decided to build malls all around the country, and these days I guess malls are popular. Once the real money started coming in my father turned into a completely different man. He started buying expensive suits and living the lifestyle of almost a James Bond character. When I was little I remember him taking me to the beach and playing ball with me, building sand castles, and getting ice cream. Well, those "humble man" days are long gone and have been for a while. I remember him telling me one time when I was little that we couldn't go for ice cream because he was afraid he would get his thousand-dollar suit dirty. After a while I just stopped asking. I guess I've got to hand it to my father. He's a good con-man, and if there is a better one in this state, show him to me and I guarantee my father has got him beat. My father still has that charm to keep my mother with him. I'm not quite sure why they stay together. Maybe misery loves company.

I pull up to school twenty minutes before the bell rings. All my friends see my car pull up and instantly run to me. My best friend Wyoming runs up to me and hugs me ecstatically. I have known Wyoming since the second grade. She gave me one of her first Louise Vuitton backpacks and we have been inseparable ever since. Wyoming is who I would want to look like if I were not me. Her blonde hair complements her blueish green eyes and tanned skin. She is somewhat like me, always having the newest and most expensive bag and always looking her best. "I can't believe you and Trent are going to be our class's king and queen!" she squeals. "Well, I mean, they haven't told us who won yet but I'm so sure that it's you two. No one in our class is as hot or popular as you guys." I look at her with envy as I notice her wearing a yellow dress that I lent her last week.

"I hope she doesn't look prettier than me," I repeat in the back of my mind. As I mutter the words under my breath I see our class nerd Dina out of the corner of my eye. I don't really know how she became the class nerd. All I know is that she does a lot of volunteer work and wears the frumpiest clothes I have ever seen. I start laughing at her and direct Wyoming's attention to her. "Hey, four eyes!" she yells. We both laugh and start hopping to class. As I pass Dina I knock her books over and laugh even harder. "Hey, ever heard of a hot iron or a dry-cleaning service?"

I chuckle even harder and grab Wyoming's hand. I peer into Wyoming's eyes. "After I win homecoming king and queen everything in my life will be spectacular!" I grin and feel my inner excitement begin to develop. "Then after I graduate from high school and Trent goes to law school, him and I will be married and on to the presidential trail! Then I can get away from my disgusting parents." "Oh, your mother was drunk again and your dad off with his girlfriend?" Wyoming replied. "Unfortunately, yes." I look away, pushing back the tears. "Who cares?" Wyoming snaps back. "Just spend more of their money, that always helps!" She tilts her head back to giggle. "Oh, if it could just be that easy," I think to myself.

I begin to daydream about Trent and I getting married and waving from the front lawn of the White House. I envision us with perfect smiles, our arms draped around each other. As the light bulbs and cameras flash I envision my perfect Jackie O outfit printed in every magazine. I smile and sigh to myself. "In time things will be perfect," I repeat to myself as we both walk to class.

Boy, was I ever so wrong.

CHAPTER 2

I sit up in my Spanish class, which is the last class of the day. I tap my pencil on my desk, eyeing the minute hand swirling around the clock. It hits three o'clock and the bell rings. I rush out of my class to my locker to go and pick up my pom poms and bag. As I open my locker I see a handwritten note from Trent. "Tonight's the night to be crowned king and queen, xoxo, Trent." I get excited and smile. I have cheerleading practice before our homecoming game. I grab my pom poms, water, cellphone, and snack and rush out to the field. "Tonight's the night for me to be queen!" I grin widely.

As I walk out to the field I see Wyoming at the top of our cheerleading pyramid shouting, "GO, RED AND BLUE, GO!" I drop my bag on the side of the field and run to my squad. I press play on the CD player and everyone jumps into formation. Music blasts from the speakers as I bounce around with enthusiasm to our practiced dance routine. I see Trent from afar in his football uniform eyeing me. He's supposed to be practicing his plays with his teammates, but with the grin on his face anyone and everyone can tell that his attention is strictly on me. How could it not be? I'm the hottest girl on our squad.

His coach sees Trent's distracted behavior and screams at the top of his lungs: "HELLO, ROMEO. EARTH TO ROMEO!" Trent doesn't even break his gaze. "HELLO, NUMBER 32!" the coach yells and throws his playbook across the field. "If I have to remind any of you jackals how important tonight is again, it's just gonna give me a down right heart attack! Not only will you upset my wife, but you will also upset the football recruiters that will be here tonight! And you can all thank Trent for his little love games he's been performing over there for this one. Everyone take a lap and give me twenty!" The whole football team tap Trent's helmet as they run around the field. "Thank God,

I'm not a guy," I think to myself. "That looks like too much manual labor."

We finish the routine and all sit down in a circle to eat our snacks. The buzz around all the ladies is tonight's king and queen. Samantha yelps, "I know it's you, Pearl, it has to be!" "And when they crown you," quirks Jenny, "make sure to smile and wave the whole time you are up there. You gotta represent our cheerleading squad with dignity and class." I look at all of them, smile, and begin to perform my best Miss America. Everyone around me begins to clap and cheer, "Go, Pearl!" "Woohoo, bringin' that sexy back!" A couple of the girls start dancing to their own beat. "Go, Pearl. Go, Pearl, go, go, go, Pearl!"

"OKAY, LADIES, that's quite enough funny business!" our cheerleading coach jeers around the corner, holding a whistle in her mouth. She is an unmarried forty-year-old vegan who is always on time. "If I've told you once or even twice, stop that monkey business! You are to be well-mannered ladies while wearing these school uniforms representing Wentworth High. Now if I can all have your attention for the first line of business." All of the girls sit in front of Ms. Timbs, on edge, waiting for her next words.

Ms. Timbs is our overly well-mannered cheerleading coach who for the last year has been trying to groom us into "polite young ladies," so to speak. But we all are perfectly aware of who we really are. All of the girls on our squad pretty much have a boyfriend, meaning that we all have experienced somewhat of the "birds and the bees." Wyoming is somewhat of the rebellious type. She lost hers last year to her ex-boyfriend. Unfortunately, he became her ex-boyfriend when she found out he gave her chlamydia. Wyoming called me on the phone one weekend while I was at the spa, crying hysterically. "Pearl, it's Wyoming. I can't believe that my first experience gave me chlamydia!" I could sense the tension in her voice. "I dunno what to do, but I know that it's so over between me and Ben!" That night she broke up with him, and we swore to never to speak of the incident ever again.

"Now, ladies, listen up. Tonight is one of the most important nights of your cheerleading careers," Ms. Timbs's voice speaks sternly.

17

"Now I want you all to focus on each one of the moves that we have practiced for the halftime performance. Don't mess up your counts with the steps. They need to line up with the rest of the squad. Let's focus on teamwork, energy, and our facial expressions!" Ms. Timbs claps her hands twice. "Oh, and please, Wyoming, no mooning the crowd this time please!" All the girls laugh and smile. "No more funny business, and I mean it!" Everyone pipes down, feeling the sternness in her voice. "If we wanna make it to state this year we need to get more serious. Now let's do this right tonight. Oh and, Pearl, good luck with becoming queen. I'm sure this is a chance of a lifetime." Our squad breaks and Wyoming and I rush to the locker room to get ready for the game.

The night is crisp and cool and the stands are packed with an audience. Standing on the sideline I can see Trent gearing up for the game. I smile at him and he waves a "hello." I quickly peer through the stands looking for my parents already knowing they are nowhere to be found. My mother told me the night before that she and my father had a very important dinner with the city mayor and his advisors. Something on the means of them donating large amounts of money toward his campaign. By this time in the evening I already knew they were having dinner, my mother probably already drunk.

My parents have never come to any of my events and I prefer it that way. Since I was a little girl I always remember my mother showing up wasted to my gymnastics competitions while my father hit on anyone and anything that moved. Sometimes I wonder why they even had me.

I shake myself out of my train of thought as I hear a voice behind me yell, "OKAY, READY, LET'S GO!" All the girls jump into formation. "LET'S GO, RED AND BLUE. LET'S GO, RED AND BLUE!" The crowd cheers us on while we all perform a backflip. "LET'S GO, RED AND BLUE. LET'S GO, RED AND BLUE! C'MON, TITANS, LET'S GO!" We all land our last pose and smile boldly. The crowd stands in an uproar as the whole football team rushes onto the field. We all grab our pom poms and start to chant: "Red and blue, let's go! Red and blue, let's go!" The crowd cheers and stomps on the bleachers as our football team lines up to stretch.

"Go, Titans!" I yell, keeping an eye on Trent. One of the girls on my squad has a crush on him, but unfortunately he is mine. I stare her down as she stands in awe of him. Trent and I have been going out for two years. I consider the two of us high school sweethearts. One day we will get married and Trent will run for president. I have my life all mapped out, exactly where to go and how to do it. Funny how some things can change.

The score is 20-10 and we are winning. The closer it gets to halftime the more excited I become. "I can't wait to be queen!" I squeal in the back of my mind. Ms. Timbs directs me to the sideline where all the homecoming candidates are already lining up for the halftime presentation. I can feel the cool, crisp air blowing upon my face like a wave of peace. I start sizing up my competition and wonder to myself if any of the other hopefuls could beat Trent and I out of king and queen. "Most likely not," I reassure myself.

I start to criticize the people standing around me in my head. "He's too short and her shoes don't match her gown. She probably bought them cheap," I laugh to myself. The halftime buzzer rings and I look up to see Trent running toward me. He scoops me up and hugs me. "Hey, babe, did you see my touch down? Boy, am I fast!" "Of course I did. It was awesome. You could run circles around those guys." Trent grabs my hand and kisses it. "Here we go." He pulls me onto the field following the other candidates. "Don't worry, we got this one, babe," he whispers into my ear.

All I can see are the bright lights shining on the field and various shapes and colors in the stands. I can't really make out any of their faces, but I can hear by the sound of all the cheering that the crowd is ecstatic. I can hear my squad yelling hysterically: "Go, Pearl, go!" "Go, Pearl, go!" I smile and wave at them. Wyoming jumps up and down in excitement. As we all walk to the middle of the field I see Dina in the corner of my eye wearing another one of her monstrous attempts to put somewhat of an outfit together. I stick out my tongue at her and make a funny face. "I can't stand frumpy people," I say to myself. "But hopefully she voted for me."

By the time we all make it to the middle of the field our school principal is standing there holding a long white envelope. Deep down inside I knew that the winner to this race of popularity was scribbled on a piece of paper and held by Mr. Wildes. Our principal is a short stalky man with a handle-bar mustache and oversized glasses. Sometimes when he gets in front of extremely large crowds he will begin to stutter.

We all form a straight line across the field. By now my heart is racing and I have one hand behind my back with my fingers crossed. "Please, please, please, let it be me..." Trent squeezes my hand. Mr. Wildes clears his throat as he lifts the microphone to his mouth. "Welcome, students, parents, and-and fellow football fans!" The crowd cheers loudly. "Tonight is a very special night and I welcome you all. It is such a special occasion to have two very competitive football teams playing tonight on this very field." Mr. Wildes clears his throat again and adjusts his eyeglasses. "I would have to say, years ago I would have never thought tonight would be as exciting as it is. We have a wonderful homecoming court presented to you and tonight is the night we find out who is your king and queen."

The front row in the crowd begins to stomp on the bleachers and chant loudly: "TRENT, TRENT, TRENT, TRENT!" The crowd goes wild and Mr. Wildes motions for them to settle down. "Now then, the students have chosen as your king and queen of Wentworth High..." My heart feels like it would drop to my stomach as I close my eyes. "Mr. Trent Dayton and Ms. Pearl Cardello!" The crowd begins to jump up and down and I can see some people shaking each other in excitement. Trent pulls me close to him and hugs me firmly. "I knew it was us," he says as he looks into my eyes.

My heart begins to flutter like a sea of butterflies and I realize this exact time and place was where I am supposed to be. All of my problems with my parents seemed to float away. The fact that they did not have the right size sweater that I wanted so badly at the mall last week drifted away into the back of my mind. Two cheerleaders from my squad walk up behind us and place robes around our necks and crowns on the top of our heads. I smile and wave into the direction of Ms. Timbs. She motions me with a smile and a double thumbs-up. The crowd yelps, claps, and sounds off in a wave of noise against my ears. The guy from the student yearbook snaps our picture and I have a quick vision of Trent and I standing in front of the White House. "In due time, it will all happen as I have strategically planned," I say to myself.

We win the homecoming game that night, making my night a double whammy. Wyoming and I hop into my car, roll the windows down, and blast the music. As we pull out of the football field we can hear people honking their car horns in excitement and yelling in the air: "Oh yeah, Titans for life!" We pass by the bus stop and see Dina sitting waiting for the bus. I stick my head out the window and yell "Hey, frumpster, or should I say dumpster!" Wyoming and I make eye contact and giggle.

"Hey," Wyoming begins to talk. "We're going out this weekend, right?" "Sure," I reply. She begins to speak faster. "Remember that guy Johnny who got expelled last year who is totally hot? Well, his parents sent him to a private school outside of the state, but I guess he'll be visiting this weekend. Which means maybe this time I can make out with him before he gets shipped away again." She turns toward me and grins and speaks even louder, "I guess one of his friends is having a party, so it should be off the hook." I can tell from the excitement in her voice that this party will require some serious retail therapy in the morning.

I drop Wyoming off at her house and see that her parents are having another one of their extravagant parties. She jumps out of the car and slams the door behind her. I pull out of the driveway and yell, "Hey, hot chick, I'll pick you up tomorrow night at 7:00 p.m., then we'll be off to see the man of your dreams!" I hit the gas and my tires squeal down the street. I can still hear the music blasting and the people partying at Wyoming's house. "Just another day in the life of the rich and famous," I say to myself as I smile. I turn up my radio and start singing to the music. "Oh yeah, life is good, nothing can bring this train down. This life of mine will keep going until the end, my train won't stop for nothing, wo-oh."

I pull up to my house, lock my car, and run into the house. I can hear my mother singing to the Beatles in her bedroom and I quickly tiptoe past her room and lock my door. "No sense in disturbing the drunken Botox beast," I say to myself. I sit down and look in the mirror. I place my crown on the top of my head and start to wave. "Tomorrow is gonna be one of the best days of my life." I smile in the mirror and am somewhat amused at what I see. "Tonight was great, but tomorrow will be even greater." I slide on my pajamas and slip into bed. Sleep can't come fast enough for me. And then there is darkness.

CHAPTER 3

I pull up to the valet at one of my father's malls. The valet guy quickly recognizes me and runs up to my car. I jump out and throw him the keys. "Well hello, Ms. Cardello." He smiles from cheek to cheek. I can sense from the sweat dripping down his face that the mall is packed today. My car gets parked at the front of the line, as it always does. I hurry into the mall and realize I only have a couple of hours before I need to pick Wyoming up. I run through the mall trying to asses a quick game plan in my head. "Okay, first I need some white jeans and a somewhat dark top," I mumble this to myself as I quickly but thoroughly window shop each store within my vision. I recognize a purse in the window that I just saw in the most recent *Vogue* magazine. I run in and purchase it.

"Thank you, Ms. Cardello." The saleswoman smiles at me while she hands me my bag. "See you next time, Ms. Cardello." The manager of the store stops helping one of the customers to run up to me and shake my hand. His face is shiny and he smells like Old Spice, I also notice that it looks like his toupee is about to fall off of his head. I fake smile back at him and walk out.

I take no less than ten steps outside of the store and see my outfit for tonight in the window next door. I grin from ear to ear and feel excitement in my stomach as I walk into the store. "Well hello, Ms. Cardello, how may I help you?" It's Theresea, the saleswoman who always helps me. She knows my exact measurements and always keeps some of the best outfits in the back of the store waiting for me. What can I say, she's got style. I point to the mannequin in the window and she nods quickly. She runs to the back of the store and comes back out already zipping the outfit into a classy dress bag. I point to some shoes I see on top of a glass table and motion to her that I want them. She nods her head.

"Your total today, Ms. Cardello, is $1,500.13." I dig through my purse and hand her my black American Express and place my sunglasses over my eyes. I sign on the dotted line and am good to go. Theresea walks around the counter and hands me my shopping bag. She brushes her sleek short black hair away from her eyes as she says, "Thank you, Ms. Cardello, and tell your father I said hello." I give her an awkward look and realize she is sleeping with my father. I snatch my bag from her hands and run out of there. I leave the store wondering how long my father and Theresea have been dating. I wonder if he has taken her on any trips around the world and what restaurants he has taken her to. Probably none of the ones he has taken my mother to. "No time to ponder about my father and her, I need to get home and get ready."

I step out of the shower and I turn up the lighting in my bathroom. I spread my makeup out onto the countertop and examine my face. I notice my clear skin and smile. "Tonight is gonna be an awesome night." I have already set my hair in hot rollers and begin with my eyes. I make them smoky enough to be noticed but not so I look like a street walker. I dust some bronzing shimmer across my face and chest and apply a light layer of blush atop my cheeks. I curl my eyelashes, apply a couple of strokes of mascara to my lashes, and spray my hair with some hairspray. I take two steps back and admire my work of art. "Man, I'm good," I think to myself. I guess some would say about me that I am rich, vain, self-centered, and snooty. But guess what? I don't care what anyone else thinks about me.

I hear my cellphone ring and screen the call. It's Trent. I press a button on my phone to silence the ringer. I realize in that moment how much I love my boyfriend but I love attention from other guys even more. "He doesn't need to know that I'm going out. There could be some really cute guys at this party tonight." I almost feel guilty for a slight second but my train of thought is interrupted by loud screams coming from the kitchen. Once again it's my mother and father having another one of their screaming matches.

I already know the drill. My mother will desperately beg my father to take her out tonight, but my father will insist that he has another "really big business" meeting with some Chinese businessmen. If I walk downstairs I already know that my mother will be dressed in one of her lavish gowns sitting at the kitchen table sipping a martini with a sad face. My father will be smoking a cigar with one of his hands resting upon his favorite red pair of suspenders. Eventually my mother will start crying and my father will walk over to her, rest his arm on her shoulder, and say, "C'mon, pretty kitten, I will be home early tonight, don't worry." Then my mother will start crying hysterically as he walks out the door, revs his Ferrari, and peels out of the driveway. My mother and I both know that there is no business meeting, and I definitely know that there are no men from China. My father is taking out one of his many girlfriends. I sigh and wonder why my mother puts up with it.

My cell phone rings again and I pick it up. It's Wyoming. "Hey, Pearl, when are you gonna get here?" I tell her I am leaving now. I hate seeing my mother drowning her sorrows in alcohol. I clip the tags off the outfit that I purchased at the mall earlier and slide my jeans on. Perfect fit. The top slides on me like a leather glove. I step in front of my full-length mirror, which covers one whole side of my room. I love seeing myself at every possible angle. My outfit hugs my body in all the right places. I do a half turn and wink at myself in the mirror. I grab my car keys and purse and am out the door.

I run down the stairs and hear my mother yelling my name, "Pearl, Pearl!" I glide into the kitchen and see my mother sitting at the kitchen table, her mascara is streaming down her face and onto her dress from her tears. But she doesn't care. "It's all your fault, you stupid girl!" I can tell by the looks of it that my mother is drunk. Her right hand has a half-empty martini glass in it. I can see two small olives floating back and forth at the bottom of it. As she sways side to side in the chair she repeats herself, "You stupid girl, it's all your fault!" I don't know what she is talking about. As I ponder the thought I see her right arm swing back in a motion that she is about to throw her glass at me. I duck down and the glass shatters above my head. She starts crying frantically as I run out. Zelda quickly runs in to console my mother. She gathers her in her arms and starts stroking her hair. "It is oookayy, Mrs. Cardello." Her Spanish accent is heavy and carries weight. "Mr. Cardello will be home very shortly, evvverything will be ookay." My mother is a heap of fabric sitting at the table. "I can't take this," I murmur to myself as I walk out the door.

I pull up to Wyoming's house and she is already outside waiting for me. She jumps and waves as she runs to the car. She is wearing a sherbet colored top and dark denim jeans. When I look at her face I realize that my makeup looks way better than hers. She starts talking as soon as she sits down in my car. "So Johnny told me that a couple of his friends will be there and they are totally cute." She grins and keeps talking. "I hope you like bad boys because Johnny's cousin just got out of jail." She chuckles. "I know it sounds bad, Pearl, but he's totally harmless, Johnny promised me." "Whatever." I say. I can't seem to get my mind off of the martini glass episode that just happened at my house. My mother would be a great character on a television soap opera.

Wyoming types the address of the party into my navigation system and we are on our way. I turn onto the freeway and roll the windows up. The music is blasting as we sing out loud while driving down the freeway. "Take next exit and turn right, please take next exit and turn right," my navigation repeats itself in its best robot voice. I veer off of the freeway and turn right. We pass by a gas station with bars on the windows. "So this must be where all the people from jail live." Wyoming laughs at my comment. "Turn right on McGee Avenue and take your first left, destination is on your left-hand side."

We pull up to the house and see a stream of cars parked alongside the road. We can hear music blasting from the inside. I park my car and we get out. As we walk across the front lawn we see crushed beer cans scattered all over the yard. We can hear voices coming from the backyard. We walk to the backyard and see a huge skateboarding ramp set up. A couple of guys wearing helmets and holding skateboards drop onto the ramp. Cheering comes from all parts of the backyard.

Johnny runs up to Wyoming, picks her up, and gives her a hug. "Wow, have I missed you." I can see a twinkle in his eye as he places her feet on the cemented ground. Johnny went to Wentworth High for about a year until he was caught selling drugs to some of the other students. And after the principal expelled him his parents sent him to an all-boys reform school in Canada. Johnny was considered one of the baddest boys in our school until he left. But as I looked at Johnny now, he still looked the same but somewhat reformed. I guess that's what happens when your parents send you off to a place like that, you get somewhat reformed.

As Wyoming was gazing into Johnny's eyes I notice a fresh tattoo on his right arm. I touch it with my finger and he twitches. "Hey, Pearl, what's up, girl? Long time no see!" He hugs me for a minute and I can see Wyoming's eyes target me. "Since when have you been into arm ink?" I try to change the subject. "Oh, yeah," Johnny replies, "my cousin Chief took me to his tattoo artist. He did it for free." Johnny turns and points to his cousin, who is covered in tattoos. He also has a large bandage but his is covering the top part of his shoulder. From the looks of it he has too many tattoos to count. Although he is considered to be the "bad boy" type, there is something kind of cute about him. I do a half wave to his cousin and turn to Wyoming and blush. "He's kind of cute," I squeal into her ear. Johnny smiles at Wyoming and grabs her hand and brings her inside.

I turn around and see Chief holding a beer; he hands it to me and smiles. "Hey, my name is Chief. What's your name?" "Pearl, Pearl Cardello," I answer slyly. "So you're Johnny's cousin?" "Yeah," he replies. "So what's it feel like to get one of those tattoos?" I sputter my sentence quickly, trying to keep the conversation rolling. "Well, it's a lot of pain, but it's worth it. You should try it sometime." I roll my eyes and give Chief my best grin. "Yeah right, my parents would kill me." We both laugh. Chief keeps eye contact with me. "Why would they kill you, do they have a problem with body ink?" "Well, my parents are very conservative, and they would never allow me back into their house with something like that embedded across my body." "Well, that's just their luck. I can't stand such close-minded people." Chief sneers and he takes another drink of his beer. He looks annoyed.

"Hey, Chief, what's up, my brotha!" I look across the room and see a guy dressed like he is in a gang. Chief walks across the backyard and bear hugs the guy. "Hey, man, long time no see. Ah yeah!"

Chief exclaims. Chief puts his arm around the guy and walks into the house.

"Once again I am left to my own devices," I complain to myself. I look across the yard and see a table with people sitting at it. It looked like they were playing some sort of drinking game. I mosey myself across the yard and take a seat. I look carelessly at one of the girls who looks at her friend. "Hi, my name is Jenna," one of the girls says. "Hello, my name is Jessica." They both smile and at the same time proclaim, "Would you like to play?" I say, "Sure," wondering what other choices I had. I peer through the window of the house and see Wyoming and Johnny making out. "Great, this party sucks and I am stuck here," I think to myself.

I start to play the drinking game and about an hour in I am in no position to walk or drive. I never thought I would be like my mother, but here I am at a table drunk, just like she was tonight. "Hey, Pearl!" Wyoming screams from the back door. "I'm hungry. Can Johnny drive your car to pick up some food?" I was too drunk to comprehend the words coming out of her mouth. "Shurrre, whatever," I stutter. Wyoming grabs my keys and runs into the house looking for Johnny. I can see her shadow through the blinds grabbing his hand and leading him out the front door. I hear the door slam and I tilt my head back into my chair. "Am I supposed to feel like I am spinning?" The words roll off my drunken tongue. Jenna and Jessica begin to giggle uncontrollably.

I rest my head on the top of the chair and look into the dark sky; the stars look extra bright tonight. My head begins to feel heavy and I can feel my eyes closing. "Hey, hey." I feel someone shaking my arm. It's Chief. "What are you doing out here passing out on this metal chair?" He chuckles a little and starts rubbing my arm. "There's a bedroom inside the house with a bed you can lie in until Johnny and Wyoming come back. I promise I'll wake you up as soon as they get here." I wobble my body to sit up straight. "You promise you'll wake me up?" "I promise." He grabs my hand and leads me into the house.

The couch in the living room has two guys already passed out on it. I step over a dog and he whimpers. Chief leads me down a dark hallway. I try to open my eyes but all I can see is darkness. I hear the knob of a bedroom door open and he pulls me into it. Chief turns the bedroom light on. I look around the room; posters of random sports memorabilia plaster the walls. The tan siding on the bathroom wall in the bedroom is ugly. I think to myself how I would never be caught dead in a bathroom like that, it was hideous. The room had green carpeting and the shades were turned down. I could still hear the music blasting in the backyard and a couple of voices still partying out back.

Chief grabs a blanket and lays it on the bed. I stumble across the room and fall onto the mattress laughing. "What's so funny?" he asks me as he takes off my shoes. "Nothing in particular, sir." I giggle uncontrollably and kick my other shoe off of my foot. It flies across the room and hits a poster on the wall of Mohammad Ali. I stare at the poster and realize that I am either drunk or the poster on the wall is moving back and forth. I laugh again at my drunken stupor and realize Chief is not laughing. Chief grabs another blanket and covers me with it; the blanket smells like a wet dog. "Do your parents know where you are tonight, Pearl?" he asks with a stern voice. "Why no, officer, but thanks for asking," I dart back at him in my best Southern accent. "If you need to vomit use the bathroom in there, and if you puke on the floor you better clean it up." I roll my eyes at him and exclaim, "Oh whatever, just let me know when Johnny and Wyoming get back!" He walks to the door and turns the light off.

Even though the lights are off and the room is pitch-black, I somehow can still see and feel the room spinning. "I drank too much tonight. Oh well, time to sleep it off until those two love birds get back."

Wyoming and Johnny should have come back but they never did.

As I lay asleep on the bed an hour passes by and a visitor enters my room. I am lying on my back and I suddenly feel the weight of someone pin me down. I jolt up in fear, only to be pushed down; my arms are pinned above my head. I can see somewhat of a shadow on top of me. At first I think it is a joke being played on me until I can feel him undoing my jeans. I try to lift my arms but he pushes my wrists deep into the mattress. This time it hurts. With one hand he has my arms pinned above my head, and with his other hand he covers my mouth. He already has my jeans down to my ankles.

I try to scream but nothing comes out. I can smell alcohol on his breath and his breathing becomes heavier. "I knew you wanted me." His voice sounds evil, his voice sounds like Chief. I try to scream again but he covers my mouth even tighter. As he pins my arms down for the last time, I can feel somewhat a hot burn on my wrists. I feel a tear fall from my eye. He groans and breathes heavy into my right ear. He gets up off of me and picks up my jeans, which have fallen onto the floor. He throws them at my face and chuckles. "Hope it was good for you, it was great for me." He walks out of the room and slams the door.

My body feels pale and stiff. My heart drops into my stomach. I feel like I am going to vomit. I turn on the light and run to the bathroom. I make it to the toilet just in time. Liquid spews out of my mouth and into the toilet. I begin coughing uncontrollably and more vomit delivers out of my mouth. For a mere moment I lose my train of thought. I feel utterly disgusted with myself and don't know what to do. I sit next to the toilet. The stench of the vomit fills the room. I realize I have just been raped. I run to my purse and grab my cellphone to call Wyoming. "This night was my worst nightmare, I need to get out of here." My cellphone beeps and I see on my phone that I can't catch a signal.

I rinse my mouth out and look down at the sink. I can't look at myself in the mirror, not now and maybe never again. I run into the room and grab my jeans. I look at the bed and see a small stain of blood. I was a virgin, how could he do this to me? Knowing that Chief just got out of jail scared the hell out of me. I decided in that moment not to tell anyone. "If I just triple lock this in the deepest depth of my memory I will never suffer from this again."

I promise myself once I get back home things would be normal. I would stay home and let my mother throw as many martini glasses at me that she wanted to. I don't care. I just want to forget about this. Pretend that it never happened and make my life go back to normal. I thought about Trent. I felt sad inside. I could see the sunrise coming up through the window. I could hear the birds chirping in the backyard. It was almost morning. I pushed the shades open and broke the screen. I jump out the window and run.

About halfway down the street I realize Wyoming has my car. I look to see if it is anywhere in sight. No luck. I can hear traffic up the road and follow the sound of it. I end up on a busy intersection and see a bus stop. The bus is coming. I cross the street and jump on the bus. I am breathing heavy and the bus driver looks down at my pants. My eyes follow his gaze. I can see bloodstains on my jeans. I can feel an emotion of embarrassment overcome me, but I don't care. I need to get home.

I ask the bus driver how to get home. He tells me where to get off and what bus to take next. "After you get off of Bus 32 you may need to do sum walkin'," he exclaims. "Where you're headed is where all those rich folks live." He tips his hat in my direction. "They don't need too much of a bus system, so we don't really travel in that direction, but you can walk the rest of the way." I decide to take my chances as I walk to the only seat left on the bus.

Women and men distance themselves away from me as I pass by them. They all look at the bloodstains on my jeans. I try to cover my face. I sit down and instantly begin to feel all the places in my body that feel pain. The motion of the bus doesn't help either. My mind begins to play over and over the horror of what just happen to me. "Please, mind," I whisper to myself, "please black out everything that happened last night. Just forget it, Everything will go back to normal somehow, I promise."

Four hours later I get off of Bus 32. I remembered the bus driver telling me it would be a long walk home, and he was right. But I didn't care. I wanted to be alone. I wanted to somehow coach my mind into forgetting everything that had happened. As I walked up the tall, narrow hill to my house cars swerved in and out of the lanes to miss hitting me. I felt like a zombie walking up to my grave. I reminded myself that if I didn't tell anyone then it didn't really happen. And if it didn't really happen then things would go back to normal.

I finally get to the top of the hill and could see my house. The sun's rays were beating upon my face and the birds were still chirping. I see my car in the driveway. "Great friend Wyoming is," I murmured to myself. I walk up my driveway only to see a catering truck unloading pastries, flowers, tea sandwiches, and champagne. One of the delivery guys looks at me and drops his flowers and glass vase. Zelda rushes up to me and pulls me into the front door. "Ooh, Madam Pearl, where have you been?" She breathes heavily. "Your mother has been looking for you all morning. Did you forget about the champagne brunch your mother and father are having for the mayor?!"

My face has no emotion as she pulls me up the stairs to my bedroom. Zelda is pulling my arm and I can feel the traumas from the night before. As we pass by my mother's room she pokes her head out and smiles. "Darling!" She rushes out and holds me in her arms in front of her. "You look horrific. Now go and wash up. Your father and I have some very important party guests arriving shortly!" She looks down at my jeans and rolls her eyes. She pushes me from her presence and snaps at Zelda. "Give that young lady a good hot bath. I don't want any of that teenage blood on my white carpet. And make sure she is presentable when you are finished. This is a very important brunch."

Zelda pulls me into the room and starts scavenging through my closet. She rushes to the bathroom and turns on the shower. She runs back to my closet and comes out of it with a gently pressed flowy dress. "Ms. Cardello, please, for the sanity of you mother, go take a shower and put this dress on. Your mother and father's party is in one hour." Zelda claps her hands twice and leaves the room.

I can hear voices downstairs and in the backyard rearranging every fine detail of the party to my mother's tastes. I can hear the clinking of champagne glasses being set up next to one another and I can hear the chef in the backyard barking for more cilantro. I close my eyes and take a deep breath. "The nightmare is now over, Pearl. You can now go back to being normal." I breathe a sigh of relief. I tear off my jeans and throw them in the trash along with the top, shoes, and even bra and underwear I was wearing the night before. "I never ever want to relive that moment ever again."

I step into the shower. The warm water drizzles down my face and it all begins to feel like a bad dream washing away down the drain. I scrub my body harder than I have ever scrubbed it before. I scrub it until my skin feels sore. I wanted anything that was on me of Chief off of me. I even considered burning the top layer of my skin off, but then decided that it was not an option.

I step out of the shower, wrap a towel around my body, and hear my phone beep. It's a text message from Wyoming. It reads: "Pearl, so sorry. Johnny and I were looking at the stars and fell asleep in your car. When we went back to the house Chief said that you left. I dropped your car and keys off at your house. Xoxo Wyoming." I instantly delete the message. I was doing good in the shower why did she have to even mention his name? I want to throw my cell phone across the room but restrain myself.

I look out the window and see the mayor's bald, shiny head from my window. I can see him diligently working the room, shaking everyone's hand and promising them some type of frivolous law that they want him to pass. I can just see the lies literally spewing out of his mouth and into their ears.

I blow dry my hair and set it into hot rollers. I quickly apply my makeup and brush a pink shimmery gloss on my lips. The sun is shining through my windows and I can hear more of the party guests arriving. Light conversation and laughter fill our backyard. The smell of food from our outdoor barbecue makes my stomach grumble. I throw my dress on and look in the mirror. I see a bruise on my wrist and instantly rush to the bathroom to apply a light foundation to it. "Nobody has to know," I tell myself. "Nobody has to know."

CHAPTER 4

I walk down the stairs into a swarm of people. I see our neighbor Mrs. Jones from across the room. She smiles and waves to me. She has some kind of fur cuff around her left arm as her right arm squeezes her younger-than-her boyfriend tightly. Her boytoy is holding two champagne glasses. Her oversized chest is almost falling out of the top of her dress, but as always she doesn't care. Mrs. Jones just had another one of her favorite facelifts a couple of months ago. Her face looks tight and has no emotion. Her forehead looks smoother than a baby's bottom and I notice that her nose is looking pointier than before. "Mrs. Jones has had more nose jobs than Michael Jackson," I huff to myself.

She dashes across the room and grabs my arms. "Well, hello, my little Pearl!" she screeches. Her underage boyfriend is walking carelessly behind her and pouts with a face of boredom. He looks at me blankly, tips his head in my direction, and forces a semblance of a smile. Mrs. Jones begins to trail on as she always does. "Now, Pearl, I heard that you and Trent won homecoming king and queen. How exciting!" She throws her arms up in the air in excitement. "How exquisite." She smiles boldly again and her face looks as if it is going to split from all of the plastic surgery that she has had. "Now, Pearl," she continues. "You and your mother must come over to my place next week for some tea and crumpets. I need to know all the fine details. I must, I must, I must!" Her overexcitement makes me wonder what type of painkiller she is taking to medicate our conversation. "And remember, Pearl, if Trent and you will be living in the White House one day, a party like this is a great icebreaker." She winks and nods her head at me. I smile lazily into her eyes and steadily agree. "Okay, Mrs. Jones, sometime next week." Mrs. Jones's laugh sounds more than overexaggerated.

Her boyfriend taps her arm and motions her toward the mayor's direction. She grabs his arm as he adjusts his bow tie. As she shimmies past me she shouts, "And remember, Pearl, don't sign anything unless your lawyer is present!" She giggles again and walks out of my sight.

I look around the room and see the more than usual crowd at my parents' party. I see Mr. Rightoff, who for the past forty years has been the main distributor of "made in China" goods in America. He has a plate of hors d'oeuvres in his hand and is talking to a group of businessmen, his arms overexcitedly explaining his company to them. "Sell, sell, sell!" I hear him pout.

I see my mother and father holding hands and walking across the room. They smile and say hello to every person they pass. My mother tightens her grip on my father's hand and walks up to me. "Okay, Pearl, you have cleaned yourself up nicely. Now don't forget to say hello to the mayor. It is very important that you say hello to the mayor." I sigh loudly. My father, eyeing a petite brunette behind me, carelessly chuckles. "Yes, Pearl, do as your mother says." The brunette and my father lock eyes. My mother tugs on his hand and begins to speak firmly. "Pearl, I really mean it, don't mess this up. If you and Trent will be living in the White House someday this connection is very important." My mother darts her eyes at my father. "Pearl," she continues, "Trent will be running for president one day, so you must get cozily acquainted with parties just like this one." My father inches toward me and taps my shoulder lightly and says. "Yeah, Pearl, listen to your mother."

As their "serious" moment passes, they turn to grin at each other. My mother grasps my father's arm and gracefully walks the both of them through the crowd and out to the backyard. My ears begin to feel warm and I can hear all types of conversations surrounding me. The noise of champagne glasses and laughter overweigh my mind. I can hear plates being stacked in the backyard and the small group of violin players my mother hired strumming away, playing their most recent song they have written. A quick flashback of the night before fills my vision and my head begins to hurt. I look at the stairway leading to my room and wonder how quickly I can run up them. "I just want to lock myself in my room and forget the last twenty-four hours," I mumble to myself.

I peer into the backyard, making sure that my parents are nowhere in sight. As I turn to make my quick getaway up the mayor slides himself between the stairs and me. "Why, Ms. Cardello, hello. Such a beautiful dress you are wearing." I give him a half nod and shake his hand. "Hello, Mr. Goldman, it's so nice of you to attend my mother and father's brunch today. Are you enjoying yourself?" He responds frankly, "Why yes, Pearl, your parents' parties are always so lovely." He places his arms behind his back and leans into me. "Now where is your well-educated boyfriend Trent, may I ask?" He has a deep and persistent voice. "His parents have been telling me about his plans for law school and his future run for presidency, how exciting!" I pause for what seems like an eternity and realize I didn't know where Trent was right now, just like I didn't know where Trent was last night while I was being raped. I begin to feel dizzy and nauseous, and somehow everything in my vision begins to spin.

The mayor cups his arm around my back. "Pearl, you look pale. Is everything all right?" I wanted so badly to tell someone. The mayor of our city was the last living person I should tell. "I need to tell someone," I think to myself. I feel an overwhelming sense of anxiety and stare blankly back at the mayor. "Mr. Goldman, I am sorry, but, uh, if you could excuse me for just one moment." I remove his arm from my back. I pick up the sides of my dress and casually make my way up the stairs.

Eight Weeks Later

"*BLEEP, BLEEP, BLEEP, BLEEP!*" I roll over and hit the snooze button. I look at the time. The clock says 6:45 a.m. I roll over again and groan. I grab the nearest pillow and stuff it under my head. "Ugh, not Monday, I hate Mondays!" I think to myself how overly exhausted I am feeling as the sun peers through my shades. There is an oak tree right next to my bedroom window. Last time I inspected it I saw a bird's nest with some eggs in it. Some nights I would sit by my window and just watch the mama bird vigorously build her nest. Weeks ago I started watching her swoop down into the yard looking for twigs to build her nest. She would hop back and forth onto the grass, inspecting small branches with her beak. I would then see her fly back up to the tree, her beak filled with small twigs and some strands of weeds. I never could understand how such a small bird could create something so complex.

The birds are chirping and singing along to the tune of the wind. I jump out of bed and peek my head out of the window. I see the nest still nestled tightly against some branches. The eggs are still there, perfectly unhatched. I grin to myself and hope in anticipation when the baby birds will be hatched. I can already feel the intense rays of the sun hitting my blinds. I decide today will be a perfect day for a sundress. I rummage through my closet. Today in my speech class I will be giving a presentation on why seatbelts save lives. I have been preparing my speech for the past week, and I have been planning my outfit for the last two weeks.

I slide on my sundress and pick up my note cards. I stand in front of the mirror and flash my best Miss America smile. "How many of you in this class wear your seatbelt every time you get into a car?" My voice sounds loud and steady. I roll my shoulders back and stand up straight. "Seatbelts save lives." I look at the clock and realize that I have been practicing my speech for the past half hour. I can smell the aroma of fresh muffins baking downstairs; the aroma of fresh blueberries fill my nostrils. I pace myself into my bathroom while making a mental list regarding my speech today. "Remember to make direct eye contact with the audience." I tap my finger on the sink counter and reply, "And don't get nervous. These are the people who nominated you to be their homecoming queen."

The past couple of weeks went by in a flash. My mother and I attended a brunch with Mrs. Jones. Her chef prepared fresh salmon and a cranberry walnut salad. My mother updated Mrs. Jones about my homecoming endeavor and Trent's presidential future. We sat and ate with her for about two hours, our conversation light yet guarded. We all settled in by her pool. While we ate, Mrs. Jones eyed her pool cleaner. Although she was wearing big dark eyeglasses I could still see her eyes darting back and forth as he ran across her backyard to his truck. Every time he would be sweating more and more, carrying various types of pool cleaners, nets, and whatever else those pool guys use. My mother and I left Mrs. Jones's house as soon as her personal trainer showed up. "Hey, ladies, anyone for a midday hike?" Mrs. Jones opened her arms and applauded Chuck, her personal trainer, loudly. "Oh, Chuck, you always know how to make me burn those ugly calories!"

As my mother and I walked down Mrs. Jones's driveway we heard her shout: "And don't forget, ladies, I'm having one of my Botox blow-out parties next weekend. Bring anyone who would like an injection of youth!" My mother threw her thumbs up in the air and nodded.

Eight weeks had gone by and the flashbacks of Chief and the horrible stench of alcohol on his breath had become nothing but a bad nightmare in the back of my mind. I realize how good a job I have been doing in keeping this a secret. I knew that I couldn't tell anyone, not even Wyoming. I decided that if I never talk about it, the memory of that night will just become another dark blur from my past. I realized that I needed to focus on the future, Trent, our relationship, and our future of him running for president. Visions of the White House fill my mind, lightbulbs from cameras flash and I get a warm and fuzzy feeling in my stomach.

"Pearl!" Zelda shouts from the kitchen. "Muffins up!" I rush down to the kitchen and see that Zelda is preparing one of her famous breakfast spreads. "Ms. Pearl, my dear, would you like a freshly pre-pared omelet?" I nod my yes but tell her I am late. "Make it to go," I sneer as my stomach grumbles loudly. Zelda rushes to the stovetop and in a couple of quick strokes my eggs are bubbling on top of a siz-zling pan. She grabs a handful of a mixture of apple-smoked bacon, cheddar cheese, fresh mushrooms, and some spinach. My mouth begins to water. I search through the plate of muffins and pick out the one with the most blueberries protruding from the top of it. Zelda grabs the muffin out of my hand and places it in a brown paper sack along with my wrapped up omelet. She tosses a plastic fork in the bag and grabs a to-go cup filled with the freshly squeezed orange juice she had prepared that morning. She hands me my breakfast and I am out the door.

As I am driving to school I try to make my best attempt at eating while navigating my car. After I almost hit two pedestrians I decide to place it aside and save it for later. I pull up to school and take a deep breath of fresh air. The sun is shining on my face as a cool light breeze gently whips my bangs to the side. I look up and from afar I can see Trent and Wyoming talking. They both look up and wave to me. I grab my bag and head my way into school. Trent walks up to me and greets me warmly. "Hello, gorgeous, what's new?" I fall into his embrace and tell him my stomach is feeling strange. "Well, I have to give a speech in about ten minutes, so maybe it is that." Trent gives me one of his infamous playboy grins and kisses me on the cheek. "Don't worry, Pearl, I know you will do great. Just breathe deep and make sure to make eye contact with your audience." He pats me on the back as he walks away, saying, "And, babe, don't forget the eye contact!" He motions to my eyes to his with his fingers and I feel somewhat relieved.

I hurry into my speech class. The bell is about to ring. Mrs. Smith is already sitting at her desk grading papers from last week's exam. "Now, everyone, please take your seats as soon as the bell rings!" she barks. Mrs. Smith is the youngest teacher in our school and was the talk among all the guys for weeks when she first started teaching here. One day I overheard a group of guys sitting at a lunch table talking perversely. "Hey, did you see that new teacher, Mrs. Smith?" They all nodded their heads quickly. "She's hot!" I walked away as they all began to high-five each other. I never did understand why guys did that.

"Now, class, I hope you all have your speeches ready." Mrs. Smith clears her throat. "This report will count for one-third of your grade, and like I said in our last session, there will be no make-ups allowed." I edge my body to the edge of my seat and start tapping my note cards on the tan colored desk. I start rehearsing every movement and motion in my head to match up with what I will be soon speaking about. I start repeating to myself: "Seatbelts save lives, seatbelts save lives. You've got this, Pearl. Remember to make direct eye contact."

Mrs. Smith motions to her desk and pulls out a list of names. "Now I have randomly selected this order, so when I call your name please go to the front of the class and do your presentation." The whole class groans as she places her hand on her hip. "Okay, well then, now that we are all settled down, Pearl Cardello, you will be the first one to warm the waters, so to speak." I feel my nerves bounce around in my stomach as I make my way to the front of the classroom. I stand behind the podium as I place my note cards slightly in front of me. The room is silent, all eyes are on me. Mrs. Smith is sitting in a desk in the back of the room. She smiles at me and motions for me to begin. "Make direct eye contact, be brave, Pearl, be brave."

I go to open my mouth to speak but no words come out. I begin to feel sweat forming on my palms, the cool air from the vent above me begins to make me feel stiff and shaky. I clear my throat and begin to speak. "How many of you wear your seatbelt every time you ride in a vehicle?" Almost everyone in the classroom raises their hands, including Mrs. Smith. After presenting the first sentence I feel my nerves calm a bit and ease into my position. "Well, I am here today to talk to you about how important wearing your seatbelt really is." I push my shoulders back and take a step toward my audience. "Seatbelts save lives." As I am finishing my sentence I lose my train of thought. A vision of Chief enters my minds and I completely black out. My body crashes to the floor as my head hits the cold linoleum floor in the classroom.

Mrs. Smith jumps up and rushes to my lifeless body lying limp on the ground. "Pearl! Pearl! Someone call 911!" One of the girls runs out of the classroom and directly to Mr. Wildes's office as some of the students are frantically dialing 911 on their cell phones.

I don't recall hearing anything or feeling anything until I wake up in the hospital bed. My body is hooked up to numerous machines that beep and purr while an IV inserted into my arm is pumping some type of liquid into me. I feel weak and dizzy and wake up as a nurse in purple scrubs is frantically pacing around the room. The expression on her face is disturbing. "How are you feeling?" she asks me as she looks into my eyes. I begin to cough and the nurse rushes to my bedside. "Pearl, what happened?" I begin to answer her but am interrupted immediately by my morning breakfast coming up from my stomach. She hands me a blue plastic hospital bag and I vomit into it. Chunks of blueberries and bacon quickly settle into the bag. My throat feels sore and I whimper. The nurse grabs my arm and speaks quickly. "Now, Pearl, Dr. Torte is on his way, but while you were blacked out the hospital has been taking your blood and running some tests." She gives me a sigh of relief. "Maybe it's just exhaustion and nothing serious."

I move around in the bed and realize I am draped in one of the ugliest hospital gowns possibly ever made. I run my hands down the robe in disgust. The nurse props up in her chair next to me, her voice sounds nervous. "Now your mother and father have sent you their best regards. They couldn't make it, but your father has sent a car to take you home after the doctor speaks to you." I wiggle my toes and realize I am here alone. I grab the nurse's hand. "Please don't leave me." My voice is soft and weak. She cups my hand and winks at me as the doctor walks into the room.

"Hello, Ms. Cardello." The doctor is a middle-aged Lebanese man with a heavy accent. "Now we ran your bloodwork and have found the problem. Well, it's not really a serious problem." I squeeze the nurse's hand and brace myself for the worst but expect him to tell me that it is exhaustion. "Pearl," the doctor rambles, "you're pregnant." The room grows cold and silent and my face goes pale. A tear streams down my eye. The nurse shakes my hand and leaps. "Wow, a baby!" The doctor motions for the nurse to settle down. "Now, Pearl, I know at a time like this, at your age, something like a pregnancy can be a huge shocker." He motions his hand to his clipboard and shows me the test results and it reads: "blood test, patient tests positive for pregnancy." "You probably blacked out from all the stress and hormonal changes going on in your body. You need to rest and you should be feeling better in no time." The doctor then looks me directly in the eye. "If this is something that was not planned, which I am assuming at your age...well, it could have been, but if not, Pearl, you need to know that you have options." He gives me a copy of the test results and pats me on the shoulder. "Get some rest, kiddo. If you plan on having this baby you are gonna need your rest."

I crumple the piece of paper the doctor gives me and try to process what just happened to me. I direct the nurse to stuff the piece of paper into my purse. Tears start to form in my eyes, but I feel them being choked back by pure anger and rage. The nurse gently caresses my hair and whispers: "Everything will be all right, I promise."

Another nurse, wearing blue scrubs, walks into my room with a small stack of papers. "Hey, hey there, are we feeling any better?" He places his hand on top of my knee and sloppily rummages through my paperwork. "Ms. Cardello, if you could just sign these papers we can release you." He points to the highlighted areas where I am to sign my name. "Now we usually don't release minors without a parent or guardian present, but your father, Mr. Cardello, has spoken directly to the doctor and this time we will make an exception." His voice trails off into the back of my mind as I ponder the thought of the doctor telling my father that I am pregnant. He flips through the pages quickly, pointing out every X where I am to sign. I sign the last form as he shuts off the monitor to my IV. The nurse then removes the IV from my arm and places a small cotton ball and Band-Aid over it. They both walk out of the room.

My mind begins to spin out of control. The nightmare of that evening returns. I clench my fists and begin to breathe heavily. In that moment I can't even fathom any of the emotions streaming in and out of my mind. "How can this be?" I say to myself as I take the hospital robe off and put my clothes on. I slide my shoes on and zip my purse up. I don't want to be anywhere near that piece of paper the doctor gave to me.

I rush outside and see a driver sitting in a black Cadillac Escalade waiting for me. He drives up to me and hops out of the car. "Good afternoon, Ms. Cardello." His words are smooth as he runs around to my side of the car to open the door for me. I get into the car and fall into the backseat like a heap of dead ashes. I sit back and grab my black shades out of my purse. I place then onto my eyes and sigh deeply. "Pearl, how are you gonna get yourself out of this one?" I close my eyes hoping everything will somehow just fade away into an abyss. Tears begin to fall endlessly down my face. Short, dry whimpers form in the back of my throat.

I peer through the car window as the driver weaves in and out of traffic. It is midafternoon and I can hear cars honking at each other as the traffic jams begin to pile up. Beyond the chaos I look into the sky and notice the clouds drifting off and toward the sea, I want to fly far away with them, to wherever they are going. Far from here, away from this problem.

The driver pulls up to my house. He leaps out of his seat to my door and opens it. "Have a nice day, Ms. Cardello." He smiles and nods his hat in my direction. I walk into my house and run up the stairs to my room I immediately lock the door and drop onto my bed. I feel mentally and physically exhausted. I roll into the middle of my bed and pull the blanket over my head. I rub my face with my hands and slide them down to my stomach and rub it. The moment feels very weird and confusing knowing that there is a baby growing inside my stomach. I begin to cry again, but this time I start dry heaving. The tears are so heavy and I can feel my cries coming deep from within. "Please release me from this nightmare." I cry myself to sleep that night, hoping that I won't wake up.

CHAPTER 5

The bell rings as I am finishing a test in my last class for the day. I walk up to the front and lay my paper on my teacher's desk. "How are you feeling, Pearl?" my teacher asks. "Uhm, I'm doing okay." I hurriedly walk out the door and through the school's hallways. A couple of girls shout hi to me as I pass them, but I make my best attempt to ignore them and act like I didn't hear them. I open my locker and grab my pom poms. "Ugh, cheerleading practice today." I grind my teeth as I slam my locker shut. It's been a week since my hospital incident and I haven't told a soul that I am pregnant. Either the doctor told my father about the pregnancy and he doesn't care or they never even told him. I just assumed he was too busy cavorting around town with one of his many girlfriends.

I walk up to practice and see Wyoming, she waves. "Hey, Pearl, c'mon, practice is about to begin!" All the girls are sitting in a circle formation stretching. I sit down in the only space available and do my best attempt at a toe touch. Wyoming begins to speak softly. "Pearl, tonight is Friday and we have to go do something. How about going to the mall to go shopping or see a movie? My parents just gave me another credit card with no spending limit on it." I nod my head but Wyoming can see that my thoughts are elsewhere. "Hello, earth to Pearl, the space shuttle is landing. Hello, can you read me?!" I snap out of it and nod my head gently. This time I make direct eye contact with her. "Ya know what, Wyoming, I just don't feel good right now. I might just stay home and rest." She snaps her head back, this time her voice carries a bit of attitude. "C'mon, Pearl, snap out of it! What's wrong with you? You've been acting so strange lately."

I curl my knees to my chest to distance myself from her. I bury my head into my legs and feel the warm tears forming in my eyes. I desperately wanted to tell her everything. I wanted to tell her how it was all her fault for leaving me at that party. I wanted to blame her for the stench of alcohol on Chief's breath and how he pinned me down and raped me. I wanted to cry and tell her how every time I closed my eyes my mind plays pictures of the nightmare that has been haunting me ever since that day. I needed to tell someone that I needed help and I didn't know what to do. I place my hands on my face to hide my vulnerability. The tears are ready to fall but I choke them back and clear my throat. "Nothing's wrong, Wyoming, everything is fine. I just feel like I have a headache." She crosses her arms and tilts her head. "Well, you've been blowing me and Trent off for weeks, snap out of it." She turns her back away from me and starts talking to someone else.

"Sure, whatever, Wyoming," I mumble as our coach walks up to our squad shouting, "OKAY, LADIES, EVERYONE INTO FORMATION!" She claps her hands as we run to our spots to practice our dance. She presses play on the boom box and everyone jumps into their position. We perform our eight count in front of Ms. Timbs as she vicariously yells at us individually. "OKAY, JESSICA, TIGHTEN THAT STANCE!" She tilts her head and claps her hands. "C'MON, KATIE, I NEED TO SEE MORE ENERGY!"

Wyoming is performing next to me and she can see that my steps aren't lining up with the beat of the music. "Pearl," she whispers loudly. "Pearl, what's wrong with you?" I look at her with a frown on my face as it grows pale. The music stops as Ms. Timbs yells loudly, "PEARL AND WYOMING, IS THERE ANY REASON WHY YOU TWO ARE DECIDING NOT TO PARTICIPATE?" The whole squad stops dancing and quickly turns around to stare at us; everyone is silent. Ms. Timbs tilts her head in a disappointed position, waiting for us to answer her. Wyoming pipes up, "Sorry, Ms. Timbs, but I was trying to help Pearl so she wouldn't make our squad look like a huge embarrassment." Everyone giggles while Ms. Timbs screams, "WELL, ISN'T THAT A NICE LITTLE STORY. EVERYONE, TAKE A LAP!" Everyone groans and Wyoming rolls her eyes at me while she starts jogging past me. I grab my pom poms and purse and start jogging in the opposite direction of all the other girls, I start heading toward my car. I can hear Ms.

Timbs's voice loudly in the background, "Pearl, Pearl, where are you going?!"

I wake up Saturday morning with a solid game plan in the back of my mind. After I ran out of cheerleading practice yesterday I came home looking for counseling on the internet. I found a place about thirty minutes away from my house. I didn't want anyone recognizing me, so I thought it was perfect. The ad on the internet read: "Free counseling for teenagers." The web page said that it specializes in any type of counseling that a teenager may need. Whether it be an unplanned pregnancy, drug addiction, or if you just needed help with issues you are having at school or at home. At the bottom of the web page there's a picture of two gay teenagers smiling with their arms around each other. The ad reads: "We don't judge anyone, we are here to help." "Well, hopefully I can tell someone about my problem," I say to myself as I print out the address of the counseling center.

I place it in my purse and pull out the crumpled piece of paper the doctor gave me at the hospital. It has been sitting at the bottom of my purse. I thought if I just left it there and didn't read it my pregnancy would just go away. It didn't work. I open the piece of paper and read those deadly words again: "blood test, patient tests positive for pregnancy." The reality of all this seems to be setting in, but not very well. I crumple up the piece of paper again and stuff it in the drawer of my nightstand that's next to my bed. I grab a pair of jeans and a tank top and put them on. I snatch up my purse and walk down the hallway past my mother's room. Her door is wide open, her TV is blasting, she is still drunk and still sleeping. I walk down the stairs.

Zelda is in the kitchen preparing breakfast. "Well, good morning, Ms. Pearl. Any time for some homemade waffles and strawberries?" The aroma of warm buttery waffle batter graces my nostrils and I smile. "Sure, Zelda." I sit down at the counter and watch Zelda prepare my breakfast. She almost makes it look like a performance. She stirs the batter quickly and as she drops it onto the hot waffle iron it sizzles loudly. My mouth begins to water. She grabs a glass pitcher filled with her fresh squeezed orange juice and pours me a glass. She places the fresh waffles and warm syrup in front of me. "Enjoy, Ms. Pearl." She winks and slides two pieces of bacon onto my plate.

"Mm," I moan loudly in admiration. The waffles melt into my mouth as the warm butter tickles my senses. I shake my head with a pleased nod. Zelda smiles in my direction. I finish my plate of food as Zelda frantically cleans the kitchen, she knows how much of a neat freak my mother is. I wave goodbye to Zelda as I walk out the door. "Have a nice day, Ms. Pear!" She grins widely.

I hop into my car and place the address of the counseling center into my navigation system, 2732 Wayward Lane. "Travel time approximately forty-seven minutes," the navigation system barks at me. I heed the directions and pull up to the counseling center forty-seven minutes later. The building is a tan and brown rundown building. As I walk up to the door I see a sign that reads: "Food bank, free for all: every third Wednesday of the month." "What's up with that?" I feel a puzzled look stream across my face. "What's a food bank?" I begin to ask myself. "Maybe it's a bank where people can deposit their food like Twinkies and stuff and withdraw it later. Huh, that's weird. Whoever thought of that is nuts!" I reply to my thought as I walk in through the double doors.

The website said it was on the second floor, in room 213. I walk up the stairs and pan my way down the hallway, "209, 210, 211, 212," I read the numbers in my head as I pass them. I come to door 213 and take a deep breath. "Okay, this is it." I open the door and walk up to the reception window. There is a small desk with a chair sitting behind it, but no one is there. I can hear muffled voices talking back and forth behind closed doors. A short Puerto Rican woman drifts by the window and smiles at me widely. "Hello, if you could just sign your name on this waiting list the receptionist will call you in a moment to fill out some paperwork." I nod my head and sign my name and sit down.

I look around the room. The walls are covered with gigantic paintings of random artwork. The tables next to the chairs are cluttered with psychology magazines and old subscriptions of *Healthy Living*. I grab one of the magazines, only to hear my name being called from behind the receptionist window. "Pearl Cardello." I walk up to the window and see Dina sitting behind the desk. "Uh, hello, Pearl." Dina gives me a funny look. She then clips a stack of papers onto a clipboard and says to me: "Please make sure to fill out all the necessary highlighted areas on each form." I nod my head and take the clipboard. "Crap!" I snap at myself in the back of my mind. "What the heck is she doing here?" I am overwhelmed with a sense of embarrassment. "What if she tells someone at school, I'm screwed!" My hands shake a little while I finish filling out all the paperwork necessary to see the counselor.

I walk up to the window trying to sound calm. "So, Dina, you work here or something?" I can't help but to look away as I feel my face turning red. She scans my paperwork and says to me: "No, Pearl, I don't really work here, I am a volunteer." "So do you like it or something?" The pitch in my voice sounds awkward. Dina looks down at my paperwork and begins to fill empty spaces on it with numbers. She lifts her head up and looks at me. "I don't do it for myself, I enjoy helping people out, Pearl, people who are less fortunate." I squirm in my clothes, keeping my thoughts to myself. "Why would she want to help the less fortunate when she could be spending that time at the mall shopping or getting her nails done?"

I walk back to my chair only to sit down and cringe from Dina telling me about her volunteering endeavors. I grab another magazine and sink my head into it. "Pearl Cardello." An ashy blonde haired woman wearing khaki pants and a green polo shirt calls my name. I get up and walk to the door. "Hi, Pearl, how are you doing today?" She smiles at me boldly as we walk down the hallway and into an off-white painted room. I sit down in front of her desk. She closes the door and takes a seat behind her desk as she crosses her arms. She gives me a warm grin and begins to speak slowly and clearly. "Now, Pearl, my name is Michelle Olson. I have been a counselor here for the past five years." She adjusts her body in her chair and picks up my paperwork and quickly scans through it. "I want you to know that this is a safe place where you can feel comfortable talking to me about anything." She turns the pages on my paperwork and continues speaking. "Now I must also tell you that this is a safe place, but for any reason if you decide to share with me some sort of physical abuse that is happening to you or thoughts of suicide or you wanting to hurt someone else I will need to report it to authorities. Oh, and also anything pertaining to sexual abuse, whether it be rape, molestation, or anything along the lines of that." She tilts her head to the side.

Michelle grabs a yellow folder on top of her desk and places my paperwork inside of it. She sets it to the side and clears her throat. "So what would you like to talk about today, Ms. Cardello?" I slump back into my chair and take a deep breath. "I'm pregnant." The words come out of my mouth for the first time and I feel something release. My hands grasp the arms of the chair and I begin to sob loudly. Michelle's eyebrows crinkle as she nods her head. "Okay, Pearl, everything is going to be okay." Her voice sounds supportive. "Why does everyone keep telling me that everything is going to be okay?" I tell myself. "They have no clue what I have been going through." My words echo inside my mind.

Michelle sits up and opens her desk drawer while she begins talking. "Now, Pearl, you need to know that you are entitled to many options with this pregnancy." My head perks up as I speak, my voice sounding shaky. "What do you mean by options?" Michelle then pulls out multiple pamphlets tucked away inside her desk. "You can keep the baby, put it up for adoption, or even consider an abortion." She keeps speaking. "I can give you this information to help you decide what path you will want to take. I also have a number that I can give you if you decide to terminate the baby." She skims through her rolodex looking for a phone number. Michelle makes eye contact with me and lowers the tone of her voice. "Now, Pearl, how does the father feel about this whole situation, are you two on good terms?"

I debate in my conscience whether to tell Michelle or not about the horrible nightmare and how this baby was actually conceived. I think back to the night that Chief raped me and how this all was his fault. My mind begins to flashback to him pinning me down and not letting me scream. The alcohol on his breath and the carelessness of his actions. I see a vision of his face and it makes my stomach churn with hatred. "Pearl, Pearl, is everything all right?" Michelle's voice snaps me back to reality and I almost give in to telling her the truth.

But I don't. "I haven't told the father yet, I don't know how he will feel about all this." I just lied to someone who was trying to help me. I knew that I was never going to tell Chief, or anyone else either. But I didn't want to reveal to her that I was raped. I was scared of Chief, and the fact that he just got out of jail scared me even more.

"Okay, well, I can give you these pamphlets and you can read them and decide what you want to do." Michelle leans over her desk and hands me the stack of handouts along with a phone number written on a piece of paper. "We can schedule another appointment, if you'd like, for next week so we can discuss what you have decided." "Okay." My voice echoes through my ears. I begin to cry again. Michelle rushes next to me and places her arm on my back. "Pearl, it's gonna be okay. Whatever you decide, we are here to help you."

I stand up and turn to walk out her door as she follows me. We walk down the hallway and into the waiting room. I realize that her hand is still rubbing my back to comfort me. The warmth of her hand gives me some reassurance. She opens the door and reminds me to schedule another appointment for next week. As she shuts the door, I realize that I am still crying. Dina is sitting at the reception desk staring at me blankly. I look back at her and in embarrassment run out of the office. I shove the pamphlets into my purse and run down the flight of stairs. I feel that I have suffered enough pain for the day and just couldn't face Dina in my time of weakness.

I get to my car and am about to open my door when I hear someone calling my name. "PEARL, PEAL, WAIT!" I turn around and see Dina running toward me. She gets to my car and places her hands on her knees, hunching over. "Man, you're fast!" Her breathing is heavy. She pauses for a moment and then stands up straight, her words begin to come out between each breath. "I don't know what you are going through, but if you need someone to talk to, here's my number." She hands me a folded-up piece of paper, hugs me, and walks away. I get into my car, shocked and shaken. I didn't know what surprised me more, the fact that I told my counselor Michelle that I was pregnant or Dina hugging me after all of the mean things that I have done to her. I was so surprised that in my greatest time of weakness Dina, out of all people, took the time to show me that she cared.

I sit down in my car and realize that was the first real caring hug that I have gotten from someone who didn't want something from me. I turn my car on and rev the engine. I sink into my chair and begin to process everything that happened to me today. I slide Dina's phone number into my pocket and turn onto the freeway. "I need to get home and read all of these pamphlets Michelle gave me," I say to myself as I set my car on cruise control and glide my way down the freeway. I can hear the wind blowing harshly against my windshield and see a storm cloud coming from the ocean. The cloud is big, dark, and gloomy, and it slightly begins to drizzle.

As I keep driving more storm clouds begin to form above me. A release of big watery drops of rain pitter-patter against my car, beating it down. "I guess when it rains it pours." The loud sound of the raindrops echo through my ear drums and into my mind. "Where do I go from here?" I feel my heart sink into my stomach. The large storm clouds pour their anger upon us by drenching us with unfortified raindrops. But somehow in the midst of this great storm I feel a sense of calmness.

I pull up to my house and zip up my purse, making sure the pamphlets Michelle gave me are hidden and out of sight. I walk past the kitchen and up to my room. Out of the corner of my eye I can see Zelda pacing back and forth from the refrigerator and to a large chopping board placed on the countertop. I can hear the sound of pots and pans clicking together and remember my parents telling me last week that they were having a small dinner party tonight.

I walk past my parents' room and see my father looking into a mirror and adjusting his bow tie. He smiles vainly as his image looks back at him. I hear my mother in her bathroom talking to her hair and makeup artist. "Now I want big and sexy hair for tonight, Pierre, *big* is the key word here and sexy."

I roll my eyes and walk toward my bedroom, only to see two large suitcases propped up against the wall. I think to myself if my parents had mentioned to me about any houseguests we were to have this weekend. I lose my train of thought as I walk into my room and gently close my door and lock it. I prop myself onto my bed and unzip my purse. I dig to the bottom of it and pull out the pamphlets I got earlier today. The first pamphlet is an educational one about pregnancy. What a pregnant woman should be eating to have a healthy baby and how much rest she should be getting. It also talked about mood swings, they almost being like a rollercoaster, and how they are normal. "Well, that's just great," I mimic to myself as I keep reading. The pamphlet also has a checklist of all the normal symptoms a pregnant woman will experience. The list reads: light or heavy bleeding after sexual activity, the need to urinate frequently, sleep interruption, weight gain, abnormal cravings. I pull a large pickle out of my purse and start chomping away on it. "I have no clue what that means." I giggle to myself as I swallow it.

I look at another pamphlet Michelle gave me. The title reads: "What is best for you and your baby?" The pamphlet then goes on to encourage pregnant woman that if she is dealing with an unplanned pregnancy adoption is an option. I then look at one of the pictures on the pamphlet. It's of a Caucasian mother and father cradling a tiny Japanese baby. They are both smiling. "Choosing adoption is a great opportunity to give your baby the life they really deserve." My eyes pan to another picture in the pamphlet. It's of a pregnant woman. She's huge, and she has her hands on her belly and is standing in front of a window. Her head is tilted in confusion. The caption reads: "Not knowing what to do about your pregnancy could be a sign of uncertainty. Speaking to a trusted source could help." It then listed a free 1-800 number to call.

I bite my lip. I have a quick and vast image of myself pregnant and fifty pounds heavier than I am now. I cringe at the vision and start to think about Chief and how much I hated him for what he did to me. I pick up the third pamphlet, still angry. It reads in big bold letters: ABORTION. I open it. I scan through it, picking out certain catch phrases and captions. "Abortion isn't wrong, it's your choice, you have rights." It then begins to talk about how the fetus cannot even feel anything when it is aborted. I look to the left side of the pamphlet at a picture. It's of a young girl smiling and holding a stack of books. The phrase below it reads: "If you have plans to further excel in your education, an unplanned pregnancy can interrupt those plans. Terminating your pregnancy is your right." I then think about Trent, college, and our plans for him to be president. "Maybe I should get an abortion." The words sting my ears. "Maybe I can do the abortion without anybody knowing, then this nightmare will be over and I can move on with my life."

I lie back onto my bed and envision myself holding a screaming baby that I didn't even want in the first place. I pick up the pamphlet about abortion and read through it again, only to hear a knock at my door. I quickly grab the pamphlets and stuff them into my purse. "Come in!" as I jump up and unlock the door, it's my mother. She is wearing one of her overly expensive gowns. Her hair is still pinned up in curlers. Hey eyes dart directly at me. "Where have you been today, Pearl?" Her voice sounds inquisitive. I look away from her and answer her quietly, "Nowhere special." I get up from my bed and start walking to my closet. "Mother, if you're here to interrogate me on getting ready for your dinner party…" I don't even finish my sentence as my mother directs herself to me again, only this time her voice screeches. "Pearl, where were you today?" I hide myself inside my closet pretending to shuffle through my clothes. I try to change the subject. "Mother, whose luggage is sitting in the hallway? Are we having company this weekend?"

My mother walks toward my closet, inching me into a corner. "Pearl, my dear, those are your bags." I give her a look of confusion and speak, my voice trembling. "Mother, what do you mean?" She digs in between her cleavage and pulls out the piece of paper that the doctor gave me at the hospital. I am so surprised all I can see are the edges of the paperwork that she is holding in her hand. My body starts to shake and my stomach drops. My mother's words carry no emotion as she walks across my room and looks out the window. "Pearl, while you were gone today I found this." She peers out the window and shakes her head in dismay. "How could you do this to our family, how could you do this to our family name?" She sighs loudly and keeps talking. "Now with all of these very important parties I have lined up for the year I just can't have my underage pregnant daughter running around making our family name a joke."

She cups her hands to her chest and turns toward me. "Now what kind of mother would I be if I condoned this behavior in our house? What would people think?" She inches toward me. "It's embarrassing, Pearl, it really is just down right embarrassing."

She quickly walks across my room as she keeps speaking. "I have chartered your father's private jet to take you to your grandmother's house in Minnesota. You better pack warm, I heard it snows out there." She pats me on the shoulder and walks out of my room. My jaw drops as she yells. "Plane leaves in three hours, no ifs and/or butts!" She walks into her room. Minutes later I can hear her and Pierre talking about a children's fundraiser in the near future. I hear my mother's laughter chiming loudly throughout the hallway. My heart sinks.

Zelda rushes into my room with the two empty suitcases that were sitting in the hallway. She looks at me sadly and sets them near the edge of my closet. I sit on my bed and begin to weep. Zelda places her hand on my back and gently rubs it. "Ms. Pearl, it's okay." I look up at her, my eyes flooded with tears. "No, it's not okay," I whimper. Zelda sighs. "Ms. Pearl, your mother said that she wanted you gone before her party guests arrive. Please hurry." Zelda looks into my eyes sadly. For a mere moment I feel like she understands. She hands me a Kleenex.

"ZELDA, ZELDA!" It's my mother's voice screaming loudly from her room. "Please check on the rack of lamb, and hors d'oeuvres. Zelda, now please!" Zelda scurries out of my room and shuts my door behind her. I cry loudly, my emotion straining deep from within me. I feel like a stiff statue trying to contemplate what had just happened. Crying uncontrollably, I stuff anything into my suitcases and zip them up. I lie on my bed crying. I hear the doorbell ring and I already know who it is.

A man wearing a black suit, with slicked back hair, walks into my room and grabs the two suitcases. I am having a difficult time processing all this as I look at him blankly. I walk out of my room to follow him. As I pass my mother's room I can see her sitting in a chair in her bathroom. I see Pierre's fingers working my mother's hair up and down and from side to side. She turns her head and looks at me carelessly, only to quickly look back into the mirror and smile at Pierre. "Yes, Pierre, I need my hair to be big and sexy tonight." She relaxes into the chair and giggles. "Yes Mrs. Cardello, whatever you say," he answers in his heavy French accent.

I walk down the stairs and can see a black car waiting for me. I walk out the door, only to hear my mother rushing down the stairs calling my name. "Pearl, Pearl." I turn to look at her hoping she will hug me or reconsider her decision. Instead my mother grabs my purse and takes out my car keys and credit cards. She holds them tightly as she walks back up the stairs and into her room, slamming the door behind her.

CHAPTER 6

I feel a sense of helplessness, something that I have never felt before. My flight was the longest flight ever, my mind stressing every minute about what was to happen to me next. My parents have always given me an array of credit cards, cash, and some type of transportation. But now I have nothing to my name. What am I going to do?

I am sitting in the back of a black car driving through Minnesota on the way to my grandmother's house. The driver in the front seat shouts, "Ms. Cardello, we are almost there." I look out the window, and as far as I can see the ground is covered with plush green grass and is birthing heavy trees. I notice many different types of trees. Tall ones, short and stubby ones, thick and wobbly trees, their branches all blowing to the beat of the wind. My stomach hurts from the thought of the unknown.

We turn onto a narrow, secluded dirt road. We drive down the path as the trees engulf us. I can hear random tiny branches whip across the car as we pass. I look through the front window of the car and can see the outline of a house. The closer we come to it the more details of the house come into my vision. It is a frumpy two-story brown and yellow house, and from the looks of it the grass hasn't been cut for months. Some of the siding on the house looks worn down and old, and it looks as if it needs a new roof. "So this is where they must send people to die," I say to myself as I cringe. I automatically begin to panic and wonder what I can do to get back into my mother's good graces.

The car abruptly stops on the dirt driveway. The driver of the car props open his door. As he steps out onto the dirt road I see him glancing down at his shoes. He bends down and brushes the brown dirt off them and walks over to my door and opens it. I step out of the car and stand up straight. "I am gonna die here," I say to myself as he unloads my bags. We both walk up to the door and ring the doorbell. The door opens slowly and a tiny old woman with a walker opens it. She grunts loudly and says: "Hello, Pearl, your mother called me today telling me that you were coming." My driver opens the screen door and I walk into the house.

My grandma scurries past her living room, and I am surprised at how quickly she can navigate her and her walker. Everything in the living room looks brown and old. "It ain't much, but this is what your parents bought me so I wouldn't meddle in all of their business." She sets her walker in front of a large sofa and sits in it. "Now you are more than welcome to use any of the amenities throughout the house." I look around, shaking my head in disbelief. "How could my mother do this to me," I say to myself. My grandmother grabs the remote and flips through the channels. She stops it on a Vietnamese soap opera and settles her body into the sofa. "Now, Pearl, the bedroom upstairs is all prepared for you, make yourself at home."

The driver quickly grabs my bags and heads up the stairs. I can tell he wants to get out of here just as quickly as I want to. I follow him up the stairs and down a hallway with wooden floors. The ground creaks with each step we take. He walks into the room with the only door open, sets my luggage down, and walks off. "Good luck with this one." He tries to smile at me but I already know what he is thinking. "I'm gonna die here," I say it again, confirming that my nightmare has come true.

I sit on the bed and look around the room and notice that everything was wooden. Wooden siding on the walls, the ceiling, wooden chairs, the dresser was wooden, and even the soap box in the bathroom was wooden. "Pearl, Pearl!" my grandmother yells from downstairs. "Dinner's up!" I walk down the stairs and into the kitchen. I sit down in front of my plate of food and examine it. "What is this?" I ask boldly. "Canned corn beef hash and mashed potatoes. I hope you like whole milk." My grandmother places a tall glass of thick and heavy milk next to my plate. I push the plate away in disgust. My grandmother sits across from me at the dinner table and begins to speak. "Pearl, I haven't seen you in years, you look so grown!" She shovels some mashed potatoes into her mouth and keeps talking.

"So how is your greedy blood-sucking mother and my son doing?" she chuckles. I slump back into my chair and ask: "Do you have any mineral water or any fresh prepared fish?" My grandmother gives me a shunned look and replies: "Sweetie, you ain't in Kansas anymore, and the sooner you realize it the better off you will be."

She trails on. "Your mother and father decided to move me out here just before their building deals came through on all those, wadd-aya call them, mega malls?" She begins to speak faster. "Somehow your mother conned my son into thinking that I wasn't accepted in their type of society." My grandmother takes a quick sip of her milk, crosses her arms, and looks away. "And it all worked on my son. Pearl, you were only a baby the last time I saw you." She looks back at me and shakes her head. "I haven't heard from them since."

I look at my grandmother, not knowing what to say. She begins to work on her corned beef hash. She grabs a piece of bread on her plate, butters it, and takes a bite. "And quite frankly, I don't even care if I never hear from those two goons ever again!" Small pieces of bread shoot across the table and onto my plate as she shouts her sentence. I look down at the plate of food and push it even further away from me. "Now, Pearl, I'm not really sure what you did for them to send you here, but if I were you I wouldn't even go back there." Her words pierce my heart as I think about all my clothes sitting in my closet and my car in the driveway. I think back to all the meals Zelda freshly prepared for me and wondered if I would ever eat another meal like that ever again. "Probably not."

I slouch even further down into my chair as the thoughts of Trent and Wyoming pace through my memory. "May I be excused?" I ask. "I'm not feeling too well and I want to go to bed." My grandma tilts her head and nods. "Okay, but you're wasting some pretty good mashers and hash. I'll save it for you." She looks down at her plate and takes another bite of food as I get up to leave. As I slowly walk up the stairs to go to bed I wonder if this nightmare could get any worse.

CHAPTER 7

The next couple of weeks go by like a slow death creeping into my life. The more I realize where I am, the more depressed I begin to feel. As reality sets in I begin spending my days watching television with my grandma and my nights slowly crying myself to sleep. Day by day I unpack light loads of clothing out of my luggage and place them into the wooden drawer in my room. One day as I am rummaging through my luggage one of the pamphlets Michelle gave me weeks ago pops up and into my vision. It's the pamphlet on adoption. "How did this get here?" I turn it over and see the 1-800 number on the back. I pick up my cellphone and begin to dial the number, only to hear a busy tone on the other end. I realize my cellphone has no reception in this part of the woods. I run down the stairs and sit on the couch next to my grandmother's telephone. It's one of the oldest telephones I have ever seen my whole entire life.

I dial the number and get a quirky woman's voice on the other line. "Hello, thank you for calling 1-800 pregnancy, how can I help you?" I pause for a moment and forget what I was going to say. My train of thought returns to me and I answer: "Hello, my name is Pearl and I was wondering do you guys have a database to look up pregnancy clinics?" I hear a short pause and the woman's quirky voice on the other end returns. "Why yes, was there any type of clinic in particular you were looking for?" I look at my grandmother sitting upright on the couch next to me. She has fallen asleep while watching one of her favorite Vietnamese soap operas and is snoring loudly. I push the phone harshly against my head and place my hand over my mouth and the mouthpiece. "Abortion." I try to speak clearly and slowly as I repeat myself. "I need the phone number and address to one of those clinics." She then replies: "Okay, ma'am, may I please have your address or zip code so that I may look up the nearest location?" I fumble for a moment and see a piece of mail with my grand-mother's address sitting next to the phone. I pick it up and read it to her. "It's 15376 Dansbury Road. My zip code is 51768."

As I am waiting I can hear the woman on the other end typing quickly and plugging the information I have just given her into the computer. "Okay, ma'am, are you still there?" her voice is still quirky. "Yes," I reply as I pick up a pen and piece of paper that was lying on the floor. The woman on the other end speaks slowly. "I found only one clinic in that area. Unfortunately it is in the next town over but it's within a ten-mile radius from you." I thank her and write down all the information. I hang up the phone, run up the stairs, and lie in my bed. I place my hands on my stomach feeling somewhat guilty, but I am quickly plagued by the horrific memory of Chief. "This will all be over very soon," I say to myself as I sit up in my bed.

I then realize that my grandmother doesn't have a car. "Come hell or high water this is gonna happen," I mumble as I map out a plan in my head on how to accomplish my plan. I decide that tomor-row morning I will wake up and walk to the town, which is about two miles down the dirt road. "There has to be some sort of bus service or something," I think to myself. "I will just have to figure it out once I get to town."

I look out the window and see the sun setting on the horizon. A warm and gentle breeze blows through my window and caresses my body. I turn over and lie on my side still peering through the glass. I watch two squirrels chasing each other up and down a tree as a bird settles himself on a nearby branch to watch them. "Tomorrow is my next step to freedom." I close my eyes and drift off to sleep.

I wake up the next day feeling more depressed than all of the other days. I assume that it is from my hormones changing, just like I read in the pamphlet. I brush my teeth and walk to my drawer to get dressed. I pass by my full-length mirror wearing shorts and a sports bra. I turn to the side and look at my tummy. I can barely even tell that I am pregnant. I have somewhat of a subtle weight gain but nothing too serious. I stuff the address of the clinic and the pamphlet on abortion into my pocket. I throw on a T-shirt and hurry down the stairs. My grandmother is cooking breakfast and is whistling to herself.

"Good morning, Pearl, would you like some poached eggs and Canadian bacon?" "Sure," I reply as I sit down to eat. My grandmother places a plate in front of me of two poached eggs stacked on top of Canadian bacon and toast. I lick my lips as I grab my knife and fork. I look in my grandmother's direction and begin to speak. "Grandma, I think I am going to go walk to town today and explore." She shakes her head in delight and says, "Okay." I quickly finish my plate of food and am out the door. My feet hit the dirt road and I thank myself for bringing a good pair of tennis shoes.

As I begin walking along the dirt road the quietness of the trees begin to sink into me. I feel the depression and sadness kick in while I replay in my mind Chief raping me. While walking I coax myself into thinking that I have every right to an abortion because I was raped. I tell myself how much I hate this "thing" living and breathing inside of me. I feel emotions of sadness and rage with every step I take closer to town. I am walking as quickly as I can with my head hung down lowly in complete sadness. I am so caught up in my thoughts that I barely see that there is a house that I am passing. I look down and see a large African American woman in her mid-sixties wearing a sun hat and working on her garden.

"Hello," the woman says to me. I stop walking and turn to her. I am amazed that there are more people living out here in the middle of nowhere. "Hello." The woman stands up, smiles warmly at me, and sticks her hand out to introduce herself. "My name is Mrs. Betty, and you must be Pearl?" She takes one of her gardening gloves off her hand and I immediately notice her dark freckles on her nose and cheeks. "Now, now, now, your grandmother called me on the phone last week and told me that you might be comin' round here." She smiles and keeps talking. "Now, child, I'm not really one to pry, but I saw you walking for about twenty yards and that darn look on your face wasn't lookin' so good." Mrs. Betty has a thick, friendly Southern accent, and as I look into her eyes I can see that she is genuine. She has cute specks of dark freckles on her nose and cheekbones that I notice immediately.

She then proceeds to change the subject. "Not many folks be comin' around these parts, but when they do, I always try givin' them that good ol' Southern hospitality!" She chuckles loudly and places her hand on my shoulder. "Now, Ms. Pearl, I just made a huge jar of sun tea and a warm batch of homemade walnut chocolate chip cookies. You must join me." I think to myself and realize that I have nothing to lose. As I follow her down her driveway and onto her porch she keeps talking. "Now, child, your grandmother used to always come over for my famous sweet tea and cookies, but ever since she got that walker I ain't seen her no more." Mrs. Betty's face makes a sad look as she keeps talking. "Boy, do I miss those days. Now, child, when you see your grandma tell her how much I miss seeing her round here. Those phone calls just ain't the same as seeing her face-to-face."

Mrs. Betty points to a chair and motions for me to sit down. As I sit down she walks into her house. She returns with a plate of cookies in one hand and two cups of sun tea in the other. She places them on the table and sits down across me. I try to inch my chair away but realize that it is bolted into the ground. Mrs. Betty chuckles. "Oh, sorry about those darn chairs. Leonard, my husband, had to bolt those onto the deck after the heavy storms kept blowing them away." She laughs loudly. "Oh, my dear Leonard. One day, sweetheart, we will be together in heaven." She takes a sip of her tea and says, "Leonard, my late husband, passed away last year. It was really nice to have your grandmother pass on through here to keep me company, but things have changed." Mrs. Betty picks up the plate of cookies and smiles. "Eat up, Pearl, while they're nice and warm. I will send some home with you to give to your grandmother."

I bite into one of the homemade cookies. Creamy warm chocolate erupts in my mouth as large chunks of walnuts crunch between my teeth. "Mm, these are delicious!" I exclaim. I smile at Mrs. Betty and shake my head in appreciation. Mrs. Betty smiles back. "Now, child, where you be walkin' to today lookin' all sad and lonely?" I pull the piece of paper out of my pocket and read the address to her hoping she won't know what it was, but I needed information. "Is there a bus that goes through town in that direction?" I shove the piece of paper back into my pocket. "I need to get to this address today."

Mrs. Betty leans back into her chair. "Oh, child, that place be far, but guess what, I be heading to a place right nearby there. How 'bout I give you a ride?" My body perks up in my seat and I feel rather lucky. "Okay," I say as I shove another cookie into my mouth. "Now drink up then. We be goin' real soon, and I hope ya don't mind but I gotta make one stop before I drop ya at your place. It's on the way." Mrs. Betty gets up from her chair. "Pearl, I must change my clothes before we leave, come on in and make yourself comfortable."

I follow her into her house and she leads me into her living room. "Now, child, sit yourself here in this living room and make yourself comfortable while I get ready." She walks out of the room. I instantly walk up to a shelf with an array of framed photographs sitting on top of it. I inspect each photo. One photo has a picture of Mrs. Betty and her late husband sitting on the exact couch that is in her living room. They have their arms draped around one another as they look into each other's eyes smiling. Another picture is of Mrs. Betty holding a small baby that is sleeping, while another photograph is of her and my grandmother sitting on her deck drinking sun tea. Another picture nestled to the side is of Mrs. Betty and a very tall guy wearing a Laker's jersey. I recognize the man immediately from the television. I yell to Mrs. Betty, who is still getting ready in the bedroom. "Hey, who's this picture of you and the guy wearing a Laker's Jersey?" I thought she maybe attended a basketball game and was lucky enough to snap a picture with the superstar.

She walks out of the bedroom and clips an earring onto each ear. "Oh now, Pearl, that's my son. He plays professional basketball." She picks up the picture and glares at it as she smiles widely. "He comes 'round here as much as he can. Even though he be playin' that pro ball my baby knows he ain't nutin' but a mama's boy." She chuckles loudly as she sets the photograph back down. I notice another picture of Mrs. Betty, Leonard and her son smiling. They are all dressed nicely and are holding his jersey up in the air. Mrs. Betty slides on her shoes and grabs her car keys. "Okay, child, all set and ready to go?" I nod my head and follow her out the door.

Mrs. Betty turns her car onto the dirt road. As she begins driving she warms up the conversation. "Now, Ms. Pearl, did ya wanna talk to me 'bout why you were lookin' so slum while ya was a walkin'?" I feel the tears swelling up in my eyes and turn my head to look out the window. I pause for a moment and then speak. "Well, Mrs. Betty, I guess I am realizing how bad my life really is." I shake my head and keep talking. "I just feel like everything is going horribly wrong and I have no control over it. I just feel so lost, I don't know what to do." Mrs. Betty starts humming and then speaks. "Ms. Pearl, you need to realize that life ain't all that bad, that's just the good Lord tryin' to wake ya up, consider it a blessin'."

We drive by an out-of-service gas station that has been over-taken by years of heavy rust. She turns left onto another dirt road, which leads us onto a major freeway. I shake my head at her trying to understand what she is talking about. Mrs. Betty turns her head to me and smiles. "Darlin', the good Lord giveth and the good Lord taketh away." She hums another couple of notes and speaks again. "Child, when I start feelin' down on life I believe it's God calling me to pour into someone less fortunate than me." Mrs. Betty pulls into a parking lot and parks the car. "Ms. Pearl, we're here. Now, ya can stay in the car sulkin' or you're more than welcome to join me. I think this will help." I step out of the car not knowing what to expect. I slam the door and follow Mrs. Betty into the red brick building.

CHAPTER 8

We walk through the door and into the building. My ears are instantly filled with the sound of various monitors beeping throughout the hallway and I realize that we are in a hospital. A nurse wearing Care Bear scrubs and smiling rushes past Mrs. Betty and shouts: "Hey, Mrs. Betty, are you here for your weekly visit? So happy to see ya!"

I follow Mrs. Betty down a long hallway and notice that there are rooms on each side of us. Some of the doors to the rooms are open and some of them are shut. As I follow her quickly down the hallway I peer into each room as I pass by them. I see a young girl who looks to be about five years old hooked up to various IVs and monitors. She lies in her hospital bed lifeless.

We walk past another room and I see a very small boy in his bed holding a teddy bear. His head is bald and is wrapped with heavy gauze. He hears the sound of our footsteps and turns to look out at us. I tap Mrs. Betty on the shoulder. "Is he gonna be okay?" She nods her head yes and keeps walking. She leads me into a small room filled with children waiting for her. As she enters the room all the children yell her name. "Yeah, Mrs. Betty is here!" All the kids run to sit down in front of a chair. Mrs. Betty grabs one of the books on the shelves and sits down in front of them. All the children clap their hands in excitement. A nurse wearing light pink scrubs sets a small chair next to the group of children and motions for me to sit down. As we all settle in a nurse pushes a little girl in a wheelchair into the room to join the group. The little girl claps her hands in excitement.

I squirm uncomfortably in my chair and wonder what I got myself into. As I look around the room I notice that each child has a hospital bracelet on their arm. Some children have a cast or brace on certain body parts while others had no hair on their head, even some of the girls. Mrs. Betty props herself up into her chair and picks up the book that is sitting on her lap. All the children smile in anticipation. Just than a tall, lanky fellow wearing dark blue scrubs wheels another small boy in a wheelchair across the room and places him right next to me. I look at the small boy and recognize him from when we were walking through the hallway just minutes ago. His small and narrow face turns toward me and smiles. His two front teeth are missing, and I can see the new ones are coming in. His big bold blue eyes catch my gaze as he claps his hands in excitement. "Yeah, story time!" He bounces up and down in his wheelchair and crosses his legs.

Mrs. Betty clears her throat. "Now, children, are we all ready for story time?" "Yes!" squeaky shouts from all across the room as all yell in unison. Mrs. Betty holds the book in front of her and raises her voice. "The name of this book is: *Don't Be Scared!*" The children wiggle in their seats as Mrs. Betty creates different voices for each character in the book. Random giggles and shouts float throughout the room as Mrs. Betty turns each page.

The little boy in the wheelchair grabs my hand and places it on his armrest as he turns to me to speak. "Hi, my name is Alex." He smiles widely and I notice his teeth again. "This part of the book scares me. Can I hold your hand?" He whispers as he squeezes my palm tightly. I look at Alex as he is enjoying the story and I can see stitches through certain parts of the gauze that is wrapped around his head. I watch while he bounces up and down in his wheelchair as he reads along to the story. Alex's hand is small and warm and I can feel an extraordinary amount of life pulsating through this young boy's hand. As Alex holds my hand I realize that I am holding his hand back as well. Something inside of me wanted to pick Alex up and hold him in my arms and tell him that everything will be all right. I choke back tears as I examine his freshly shaven hair on the side of his head. I hold Alex's hand until Mrs. Betty finishes the last page of the book.

As all the children clap, Alex turns to me smiles and says, "Don't worry, it's never as bad as it looks." His words pierce my heart. The tall, lanky man comes up behind him and wheels Alex out of the room. I stare into my hand noticing that Alex has placed something in it. I open my palm to see a small cross shimmering in the light. I look back but Alex is already gone. Mrs. Betty walks up to me and says, "We best be goin' now, Ms. Pearl. I don't want cha late for your appointment. I would be stayin' longer but today I'll make an exception."

We walk out of the room as another nurse sits down and prepares another book to read for the children. As Mrs. Betty and I walk down the hallway I try and remember what room Alex was in. As we pass one of the doors, I peer through it and see Alex sitting on his hospital bed. I turn to walk in but realize he isn't alone. I stand in the doorway as I watch him sit on his bed. A nurse walks up to his bedside and injects a needle into one of his IVs. The nurse then lays Alex onto the bed as she quickly injects three needles full of medicine into Alex's bloodstream. Alex turns his head toward me and waves. He has an undying smile upon his face. I want to walk into the room but am paralyzed by my own fears of not knowing what to say to him.

Mrs. Betty taps me on the shoulder. "We must be a goin' now, Ms. Peral." I walk out of the room with my head hung low in shock. "What's wrong with all those kids?" I ask Mrs. betty as she pulls out of the parking lot. "Ms. Pearl, all those children were born with some type of illness." She shakes her head. "Now, not one of those children never seen nothing outside those hospital doors. They were born in a hospital and they ain't never seen nothing else."

I look out my window as we drive past a diner packed full of patrons sitting down enjoying their meal. A smiling waitress wearing a bright yellow shirt places two pieces of pie down on top of a table as her customers grin widely. We drive by a park and I see two children running on the grass playing with their dog. As they run they laugh uncontrollably as their dog prances beside them. Mrs. Betty pulls up to a solid brown brick building. There is no sign on the building, only a small address plaque next to a glass door. "Okay, Ms. Pearl, here we are." She parks her car and pulls out a crossword puzzle. She motions for me to get out of the car. "Now, Ms. Pearl, take your time. I be lovin' these good ol' crossword puzzles. I'll be waitin' here for ya." She laughs loudly as I slam the door and walk up to the clinic.

I walk into the clinic and sign my name onto a clipboard sitting next to the receptionist. She hands me some paperwork to fill out and tells me to take a seat. "The nurse will call you when they are ready." She smiles and hands me a pen. The walls are a dimsy yellow and everyone sitting in the waiting room looks bored. I scan through the paperwork as it asks me multiple questions. Is this your first time here? What is the reason for your appointment? I write down *pregnancy* and finish filling out the forms.

I sit in my chair and begin to think about all the children in the hospital and how brave Alex is. I think about what Mrs. Betty told me in the car, how those children have never had a normal life and how much suffering they have gone through. I feel sad inside as I remember the look on Alex's face as the nurse injected his IV with medicine.

"Pearl Cardello." A nurse wearing white scrubs waves at me from the other end of the room. I grab my paperwork and follow her through the door. She leads me down the hallway and into a small room. There is a bed with various medical machines surrounding it. We both sit down and I hand the nurse my paperwork. "Okay, I see that you are pregnant. How far along are you?" "Uhm, I'm not exactly sure, maybe a couple of months." My voice stutters. "Well, that's okay. When the doctor gets here she will give you a pap smear and ultrasound so we can see what's exactly going on in there." The nurse has me stand on a scale in the room and weighs me.

"So, Pearl, how have you been feeling with your pregnancy, any complications?" The nurse picks up her pen and waits for me to answer. "Well, I guess I'm feeling okay. I just have to pee a lot." She smiles as we both giggle. She then hands me a paper gown and tells me to undress and put the gown on. "Just sit there on the table and wait for the doctor. She should see you shortly." She shuts the door as I begin to undress.

As I stand naked in the middle of the exam room I place my hand upon my growing belly. I then think about Alex and everything that I had just encountered with Mrs. Betty. I cover myself with the robe and sit on the exam table as I wait in anticipation for the doctor to enter my room. As I sit and wait I think to myself about how much I hate what Chief did to me. Replaying that night over and over in my head has caused somewhat of a nervous breakdown to develop in my brain. I think about my parents and feel a sense of anger and rage swelling up inside of me. "I will never forgive them or speak to them again." The words swell inside of my heart.

The door to the examining room opens swiftly and a pretty Asian doctor enters the room. She is quickly paging through my file. "Hello, Pearl, my name is Dr. Tiji, I am the head doctor in this clinic specializing in prenatal care. Now, how may we help you today?" I sit up stiffly and reply, "I want an abortion, the sooner the better." As she walks toward me and motions for me to lie on top of the table, she starts to examine the top half of my body, probing and squeezing specific areas as she asks me questions. "Have you been having any complications with your pregnancy?" "No, not really. Well, maybe some queasiness in the morning, and I feel really tired." I squirm on the table as she gently presses on my stomach. "Okay, Pearl, those are normal symptoms of pregnancy. I read your chart and can see that you have a normal weight gain. Don't be afraid to gain the weight. You will need it for the pregnancy." I interrupt her abruptly, "Dr. Tiji, I came here because I want an abortion, not because I wanted to discuss my unborn baby." Dr. Tiji looks up and replies, "Okay, Pearl, this is the first examination. We will do a check-up, and when you leave today you can schedule an appointment for the procedure with the receptionist."

She motions for me to place my feet in the stirrups at the bottom end of the table. They make my feet feel empty and cold. Deep down inside I feel disgusted by the words that came out of my mouth but I had so much hate and anger inside of me that I knew that this was the only way to get Chief out of my life. Dr. Tiji then replies, "An abortion is a very standard procedure. Before the actual abortion we need to do a short mental screening on you to make sure that you will be able to deal with the after effects of having the abortion. We also have referrals to counselors if you ever need anyone to talk to."

Dr. Tiji finished the pap smear and walked around to the side of the table. She lifts open my gown and says, "Okay, Pearl, we need to do an ultrasound to see how far along you are." She then squeezes a cold clear gel across my belly and tells me to place my hands behind my head. She dims the lights and places a probe on my stomach, which somehow resembles a roll-on deodorant bottle. There is a TV screen next to my face. She presses into my stomach with the probe and says, "Okay, Pearl, try not to move. I need to get a good picture." I look at the screen not sure what I am looking for. She puts her face next to the screen. "Okay, I can see the head and the legs." I look at the screen and see a bit of an outline of a whitish blob floating back and forth. "That's a baby?" She moves the probe around even more, but this time presses firmly on my stomach. I flinch in agony. "Why, yes, it sure is a baby. No use telling you the sex of it."

Dr. Tiji then flips on the light as she wipes the clear gel off of my stomach. She pulls a handheld monitor from out of her pocket and places it on my belly. "*Ba boom, ba boom, ba boom, ba boom.*" "What's that?" I look at her with a perplexed look across my face. "I'm listening for the baby's heartbeat. Your baby's heart sounds very strong and healthy." As I listen Alex's face crosses my mind. I look up at the doctor. "My baby's heart sounds strong and healthy?" I think of Alex and all the other children who weren't born healthy and who were struggling just to survive, and here I have a healthy baby with a strong heartbeat whom I was trying to get rid of. My selfish intentions gripped me from within as a wave of sadness entered into my heart.

I looked Dr. Tiji in the eyes. "What if I decide to keep my baby, is that okay?" Dr. Tiji picks up my chart and tilts her head. "Pearl, this decision is completely up to you. I can't tell you what to do." Dr. Tiji leaves the room and tells me that I can get dressed. I sit for a moment and ponder my life with a baby. I start to feel the pressure from the unknown. I grab my clothes and get dressed. I walk out of the clinic feeling more confused than I was before my appointment. I see Mrs. Betty sitting in her car giggling away as she writes in letters to solve her crossword puzzle.

I open the car door and sit down. "Oh, child." Mrs. Betty nudges my shoulder. "So how was your meetin'?" I slam the door shut and gaze out my window. "Everything is fine. Thanks for driving me." Mrs. Betty pulls out of the parking lot and onto the main road. Mrs. Betty hums a song to herself the whole way home as I sit in silence. She pulls up to my grandmother's house and stops the car. She pulls a bag of cookies out of her purse from earlier that day and smiles at me. "Okay, Ms. Pearl, here ya go. Now I be goin' to church tomorrow in the mornin'. If ya like to join me, I can be here at ten thirty a.m."

I grab the bag of cookies as I rush out of the car, not realizing that the pamphlet on abortion has fallen from my pocket and onto the car floor. "Thanks again, Mrs. Betty. I'll tell my grandmother that you said hello, and I will be ready tomorrow morning." "What do I have to lose. I have nothing else to do," I think to myself as I slam the door and run up to the house.

As I walk into the door I see that my grandmother is passed out on the couch in an upright sitting position. The television is blasting and I can see that she was watching another marathon of her favorite Vietnamese soap opera. I turn off the TV, place the bag of cookies in the kitchen, and run up the stairs. I lie on my bed with my hand resting on my belly and think of Alex again. I look up at my ceiling and make a list of everything that could go wrong if I had this baby. I worried about where we would live, and the fact that I didn't even know how to raise a baby challenged me even more. I thought about my parents and how they turned their backs on me and how this whole scenario was because I was raped. A piece of me kept telling me how I deserved the abortion and if I just went through with it everything would go back to normal. I remembered my life living with my parents and missed it. I wondered if I went through with the abortion if they would take me back. Then my life could go back to normal. All my future plans I had for Trent and I could actually end up happening. I set my alarm clock and fall fast asleep dreaming of my old life and trying to figure out how and when I could get back to it.

Its nine o'clock in the morning as my alarm goes off to set me in motion. I jump out of bed and immediately begin rummaging through my dresser drawer looking for something to wear. I didn't know what to pick out. I had never been to church and didn't really know what to expect. I pick out a floral dress, put it on, and walk into my bathroom. My face looked bloated and my eyes were blood-shot red. "Oh great, what a nice way to make an impression. My eyes make me look like a vampire." I grab my makeup bag and begin to make something from nothing, trying desperately to conceal the puffiness around my eyes. I finish my makeup and grab my shoes. I run downstairs and see my grandmother place a plate of food down on the table for me. "Eat this. You're going to need your strength." She places a plate down which is piled high with fresh homemade biscuits and sausage gravy. She winks at me as she places a glass of whole milk next to it.

My grandmother opens her fridge and begins digging in it, her body is halfway engulfed in it. "So, Pearl, what are ya all dressed up for?" I answer her in between bites, "Mrs. Betty is taking me to church." She perks her head out of the fridge and motions me with her hand. "Aw, I like Mrs. Betty, but that's all a bunch of hog wash, if I must say so." She turns to the counter and grabs the salt and pepper and places it on the table. "Well, have fun. I'll be here all day watching my Vietnamese soap opera marathon."

She walks out of the kitchen and into the living room, where she plops herself onto the sofa and turns on the television. I instantly begin to hear a high-pitched woman on television begging some man by the name of Ben to stay with her. "How dramatic," I say to myself as I finish my plate of food. I place my dishes in the sink as I hear Mrs. Betty's car honking from outside. "C'mon now, Ms. Pearl!" I can hear her giddy voice in the distance. I say goodbye to my grand-mother as I walk out the door.

I can see that Mrs. Betty is wearing an enormous hat on top of her head. She smiles broadly as she sees me walking toward her car. "My, my, my, Miss Pearl you be looking so pertty, co'mon child you better be gettin' in this car, we must be a leavin'." Mrs. Betty pulls out of my grandmother's driveway and we are on our way. We pull into a small parking lot located on the other side of town. The church building has a huge white cross located on top of their roof. The building is a tattered brown in color and makes me realize how much of a disappointment I am in for.

I sluggishly drag myself out of the car as I drag my feet to the front door. I can hear loud voices shouting and hands clapping as Mrs. Betty squeezes my arm and smiles. "I think you'll be mighty surprised, Ms. Pearl." We walk into the church and take a seat in the last row. There is a choir standing on the stage singing as a man on the microphone dances across the stage. I chuckle to myself as he stomps his feet to the rhythm. "Holy Ghost fire shot up in my bones!" He does a quick turn and stomps his feet again. "C'mon, people, we've got the fire of the Holy Spirit in this house!" The choir throws up their arms in unison, rejoicing in praise. All the people in the audience start shouting and dancing to the music. Mrs. Betty claps her hands, shakes her body, and shouts, "Hallelujah, mighty is the Lord!"

I stare in amazement around the room at all the people singing. A woman next to me has her arms raised as tears are streaming down her face. I feel uncomfortable and slink into my chair. I cross my arms and wait for this nightmare to end. The music slows down and the whole room begins to sway. I feel a peace overcome me as I listen to the words that the choir is singing. "Worthy is the lamb. Worthy is the lamb. Thank you for the cross, Lord, thank you for the price you paid, bearing all my sin and shame. In love you came and gave amazing grace."

I don't really understand but my heart somehow feels a sense of belonging. I sway in my seat, following the rest of the room. The man on the stage lifts his hand and begins to speak. "Jesus, thank you for what you did on the cross. God, help those here today who feel that they have no hope. You, Lord, are our hope."

I think of Alex and the small cross he placed in my hand. I stand up on my feet and I look up to the ceiling thinking about the past couple of months and all the hell I went through. Tears begin to fall uncontrollably down my face. I place my teary-eyed face in the palm of my hands and weep bitterly. My mind cannot process what is happening to me as my heart breaks in the middle of this room. The music is still playing as the choir takes it up a notch. A woman in the front row of the group takes a step forward as she sings a solo. "You deserve the glory and the honor. I lift my hands in worship as I lift your holy name." The whole choir joins in, their melody sounding like a calming sound to a storm. "For you are great. You do miracles so great, there's no one else like you. There is no one else like you."

I place my hands on top of my stomach as another rush of tears fills my eyes. "I don't know if you're even real, God, but if you are, please help me." I felt the words spring up from the depths of my soul. A man wearing a suit and tie walks up to the stage and positions himself to speak to the crowd. His eyes are closed as he speaks into the microphone. "God will leave His ninety-nine sheep to go find His one." He raises his hand. "There is a woman in this room today and you are pregnant and scared. God is reaching out to you right now and wants me to tell you that He has you in the palm of His hand." He clears his throat. "You need to know that the Lord sees what you are going through. What that man did to you was wrong. God wants to heal you today of all the hurt and pain you have gone through. If you will please come to the front of the room so I can pray for you."

I feel a knot forming in my stomach and know that he is talking to me. I step out into the aisle and start walking toward the altar. I can feel my cheeks turning red as all eyes in the church watch me walk to the front. A woman comes from behind me and embraces me as I stand in front of the man with the microphone. He places his hand upon my head as he prays for me. I begin crying uncontrollably loud again. As he finishes praying for me the woman pulls a tissue out of her pocket and hands it to me. I wipe the tears off my face and head back to my seat. I feel as if a huge burden has been lifted off my shoulders. I feel as light as a feather as I walk back to my seat. Mrs. Betty hugs me as we all sit down.

The man who prayed for me introduces himself through the microphone. "Hello, everyone, my name is Pastor Troy Rivers. Welcome if this is your first visit." The whole congregation sits quietly as he opens his Bible and begins to preach. The pastor's words are sharp and direct. "For God so loved the world that he sent his only begotten Son so that whoever may believe in Him shall not perish but have everlasting life." His words pierce my heart. He then explains how God sent His Son named Jesus to die on the cross for our sins. He looks directly at the crowd and asks if anyone would like to accept Jesus into their heart. Hands go up all across the room, including mine. "Amen, God is good!" The preacher slows his words down. "Everyone who raised their hands please say this prayer out loud. 'Dear father God, thank you for dying on the cross for me. Please forgive me of all of my sins. Please come into my heart. I make you my Lord and Savior.'"

Men in suits skim across the aisles and start handing out Bibles to each person that raised their hand. A short, stout man hands me a Bible and smiles. I tuck it under my arm as the church is dismissed. As Mrs. Betty and I are walking out of the door of the church the pastor shakes my hand. "Hello, how did you enjoy the service?" "It was nice," I say as Mrs. Betty chimes in. "Pastor, this is Ms. Pearl, Anne's granddaughter." "Oh, how nice. I know your grandmother. We drop food off to her every week. Tell her I said hello." The pastor pats my shoulder and speaks as we walk out the door. "Ya know, Pearl, we have a homeless food ministry tomorrow if you would like to volunteer. Mrs. Betty helps out here also." I shake my head and tell him yes.

As we were driving home from church Mrs. Betty's voice rings in. "Ms. Pearl, would you like to join me for lunch at my place?" "Sure," I reply as we make our way home. Mrs. Betty sets a spread of turkey croissant sandwiches, potato salad, and kettle chips across the table. "Dig in, Ms. Pearl." We begin to eat our sandwiches as the sun shines upon our faces. "Ms. Pearl, I don't mean to be pryin', but you dropped this in my car there yesterday." She places the abortion pamphlet on top of the table. I hang my head down low as Mrs. Betty grabs my hand and squeezes it. "Don't worry, child, I understand."

She leads me into her house and into one of the back bedrooms of her house. The bedroom is filled with various photographs. She bends down and grabs a shoe box underneath the bed. She pulls it out and dusts it off. I sit on the bed as I wait for her to speak. Mrs.

Betty hands me a newspaper clipping. The title reads: "Jury decides man is not guilty in the raping of Betty Sealson." The article goes on, "Tommy Woodson was found not guilty in the trial of Betty Sealson due to lack of evidence."

My jaw drops as I look at Mrs. Betty. "Child, I was you forty some years ago. I contemplated abortion also, but somehow the good Lord intervened. With God all things are possible." I was surprised who her son was. The television reporters would always do interviews with him. He seemed so refined and laid back. I would have never known that his mother was the victim of rape and that he was the outcome. "What made you decide to keep him?" I ask her as she grabs a photograph of her son and smiles at it. "Ms. Pearl, the good Lord gave me the strength to forgive that man who did this to me. I had to forgive him. I had so much of that anger built up inside of me. My baby boy was a blessing from a curse. God worked it out that way."

Mrs. Betty leads me out to her porch and pours me a tall glass of iced tea. I take a bite of my sandwich and relax into my chair. "I feel so angry inside from what happened to me, I don't know how to deal with it." Mrs. Betty scoops a large portion of potato salad onto my plate and smiles. "My child, I remember one time just lyin' in my bed and crying out to God for help. And ya know what God said to me?" I sit up in my chair and lean in to Mrs. Betty's words. "The good Lord told me to forgive him, and boy did that make me mad." Mrs. Betty takes a sip of her tea. "Ms. Pearl, when you have unforgiveness in your heart toward someone or even anyone, it holds you captive. But forgiveness is a choice of letting someone go from the debt they did to you and giving them to God to deal with."

Mrs. Betty leans back into her chair. "Pearl, unforgiveness will only make you bitter and jaded. There's a sense of freedom in receiving forgiveness from God and also forgiving those who have hurt us." I take a bite of potato salad and think about Chief and my parents. Sitting on Mrs. Betty's porch and talking to her was making me realize how much I hated both of them. I began to think about all the hurtful things each of them did to me. I looked up at Mrs. Betty and asked her bluntly, "What if you don't want to forgive them? What if what they did to you was unforgivable? Don't I have the right to stay angry?" Mrs. Betty tilts her head to the side and shakes her head. "Ms. Pearl, like I said, forgiveness is a choice. I had problems forgiving that man that raped me, but with God all things are possible. Pray for the strength to forgive, and as you forgive, Ms. Pearl, God will send you a provision of healing to heal your broken heart."

Mrs. Betty smiles as she caresses my back. "Ms. Pearl, pray and ask God what to do. He is the only one who can give you the answer." We finish our lunch as the day winds down. And I feel an excitement brewing inside my heart from the advice that Mrs. Betty gave to me. I tell Mrs. Betty that I want to walk home so I could talk to God about everything that was going on in my life. She reminds me about volunteering at church and tells me that she will pick me up tomorrow.

I kick the gravel as I walk down the dirt road leading to my grandmother's house. "God, are you there?" My voice sounds shaky. "I know that I have pretty much ignored you my whole life and I'm sorry about that. But if you can find the time in your busy schedule, can you please help me?" As I walk I keep hearing Mrs. Betty's voice in the back of my mind, "Forgiveness is a choice." I stop walking and look up to the sky. "Lord, please help me to forgive. I honestly don't want to, but I know I have to. And please heal me." Tears start to fall endlessly down my face. "I just don't know what to do anymore, but I know I am hurting. Please help me."

I cry the rest of the way home and wipe the tears from my face as I walk up the steps and into my grandmother's house. All the tears I shed while walking home made me feel better inside. I felt such a peace in my heart. I still knew God had a lot to work out in my life, but I knew that with God all things are possible. I walk through the door and see my grandmother sleeping on the couch in an upright sitting position as always, her Vietnamese soap opera blasting on the television. I shut the television off and run up the stairs.

I walk into my room and close the door. I lie on my bed as my mind starts processing my day. I thought about the church and how much I enjoyed the choir. I find myself holed up in my room reading my Bible until I hear my grandmother yelling my name from downstairs. "Pearl! Pearl, dinner time!" I go downstairs and ask my grandma what's for dinner as I sit down at the kitchen table. "Homemade fried chicken, mashed potatoes, and bacon green beans." My grandmother winks at me as she places a huge platter of fried chicken onto the table. I grab one of the biggest pieces of chicken, dip it into my mashed potatoes, and shove it into my mouth. It's delicious.

"So how was church today, Pearl?" My grandmother asks me as she spoons a hearty helping of bacon green beans onto my plate. "It was really cool, Grandma. I told them I would help them serve food to the homeless people." My grandma gives me a troubled look. "Wow, okay. Well, that's so far off from the lifestyle that your parents raised you. Are you sure that is something you would want to do?" I shovel a forkful of green beans into my mouth. "Well, I guess this is somehow the new me." I stir my mashed potatoes around on my plate. "I know that living out here is so much different. I thought maybe that it would be good to try something new. Maybe God really does have a plan for me."

My grandmother shakes her head in anticipation, waiting for me to tell her that I have lost my mind. "Well, Pearl, life is what you make it. And if you believe that serving the homeless people will help you find yourself, so be it." The timer on my grandmother's oven goes off and she jumps out of her chair. "Oh, that must be my strawberry rhubarb pie. Hurry up and finish eating. I've got some vanilla ice cream to go along with this warm pie." My grandmother grabs a knife and starts cutting a piece of pie. She places it on a plate and places a scoop of ice cream right on top of it. She grabs a fork and takes a big bite. "Oh, this is what heaven must really taste like!" She cuts another piece of pie, places a scoop of ice cream on it, and sets it down on the table in front of me. She points her fork at me in between bites as she speaks. "Pearl, maybe it is a good idea for you to be helping the less fortunate, it will keep you out of trouble."

My grandmother and I finish our warm rhubarb pie and I help her clear the table. As my grandmother is doing the dishes she turns and looks at me. "You know, Pearl, I use to go to church myself. When your father was a young boy we used to go to church." She scrubs one of the greasy pans and keeps talking. "With everything that has happened, I just can't seem to get back to God. Maybe one day me and your father will come back." She looks down at the soapy water and scrubs harder. "Maybe one day, Pearl, maybe one day."

CHAPTER 9

I wake up late and have barely any time to get ready before I hear Mrs. Betty's car horn honking for me outside. I feel nauseous this morning and my feet feel swollen, I realize it's from walking home and decide to never do that again. I run down the stairs, grab a piece of toast off of the plate of breakfast my grandma made for me, and run out the door. I jump in Mrs. Betty's car and she pulls out of the driveway. "My, my, sweet child, what a gorgeous day to be alive." Mrs. Betty smiles as she starts humming a melody to herself.

We pull up to the church parking lot and I can see that there is already a line of people forming in front of the church doors. Mrs. Betty and I walk through the double doors and into the kitchen located in the back of the church. There are multiple volunteers baking fresh rolls, mixing large bowls of green garden salad, and one woman dolloping fresh whipped cream on top of pumpkin pie slices.

All the workers smile and say hello to us as we walk in. The pastor of the church comes directly up to us and grins. "Hello, ladies, so glad you could make it. We need help setting the tables out front. The people are hungry and waiting to eat." Mrs. Betty and I are handed a big box filled with plastic forks, napkins, and knives. We walk into the large room and start setting the tables. I look out the window at the crowd. A single mother with her two children are waiting patiently in line waiting for the doors to open. I look and see an old man sitting by a tree. He is wearing dirty clothes that have numerous holes in them. He places his dirty hands on his forehead. His nails are full of dirt and he has an expression on his face of frustration. I look down and can see that his knee has a heavily infected wound on it. His jeans have dry dark brown bloodstains covering his knee. Deep down inside I start to feel my heart breaking for him.

I run to the kitchen. "There is someone who needs medical attention outside!" A woman wearing plastic gloves shouts back. "Sorry, but there's nothing really that we can do." She hands me a stack of Band-Aids and some ointment. I grab a warm soapy washcloth and rush outside. I find the old man still sitting under the tree. Now that I am standing next to him I can see that his clothing and body are much dirtier than I thought. I place the warm washcloth on the homeless man's knee. He reacts loudly. "Ouch, that hurts!" I clean his wounded knee, apply the ointment, and begin to bandage it up. "Thank you, that feels much better."

As I finish cleaning the homeless man's knee two girls with paper signs run past me, shouting, "Hey, everyone, Jimmy Jenson is back from football training camp. The welcome home parade for him is in town!" The two girls jump up and down and start running toward town. I look at the old man with a puzzled face. "Who's this Jimmy Jenson that those girls are going crazy over?" The old man chuckles. "Oh, that's Jimmy Jenson. He's this town's all-American football hero. One day that boy is gonna be drafted to a pro football team."

I finish bandaging the man's knee as I look at his rugged face. I can see that the years have taken a toll on him. I think back for a moment when I lived with my parents, how much more different my life is now. When I was living with them I got anything I wanted— clothes, shoes, cars, anything. I wouldn't have been caught dead helping someone else, let alone a broken-down homeless man. I place my hand on his shoulder and say, "The food will be ready soon."

I get up to walk away and realize something in me was drastically changing. It was like the more I let God in, the more He began to change me. I enter the church as they are setting up the food onto a long table. Mrs. Betty hands me a pair of plastic gloves, a spoon and tells me to serve the spaghetti. I stand behind the extremely large tray of spaghetti as the pastor opens the church doors. He greets each person as they pass him. I spoon the spaghetti on each tray as it passes by me. When my tray of spaghetti is almost all gone a woman from behind me places another extremely large tray of piping hot spaghetti in front of me to serve.

I look at each person's face as they pass through the line. All different ages and races filled the room as they all sat at a table and ate. Nobody really spoke to one another, everybody's head hung low over their plate of food, wondering where their next meal would come from.

The pastor stands up on a small platform in front of the table. "Thank you all for coming. Right now we are praying to expand this free food service to seven days a week. As of right now we do not have the funding, but in God's timing it will be." Everyone in the room claps loudly and smiles.

A middle-aged redheaded woman hands me a tray of pumpkin pie slices and tells me to please pass them out. I realize that I have never really carried a tray of food to serve anyone. I reassure myself that everything will be okay as I pick up the tray of pie slices. I start at the left side of the room, smiling widely as I drop a pie slice beside each person. I work faster as I adapt to my new waitressing skills. I run back to the kitchen to grab another tray. I balance it on my hand and slide past the other volunteers smiling. Mrs. Betty claps as I stroll past her carrying a full tray of pie slices. My steps quicken as I walk back into the room full of people.

As my thoughts carry me into a different place, I am averted quickly as I lose my balance from tripping over my own two feet. As I fall flat on my face, the tray full of pie slices fly across the room and directly onto Jimmy Jensen, who has just walked through the church doors. The room turns silent as everyone looks at Jimmy and his shirt, which is covered with pumpkin pie filling. I look up from the floor at Jimmy as my face turns red in embarrassment.

I see a little boy from across the room point at me and yell, "Mommy, look, she dropped all of the pie!" He starts crying uncontrollably loud. "Now we don't get pie, Mommy. I want my pumpkin pie!" I feel devastated as I stand up in front of the whole room, everyone looking directly at me and Jimmy. Jimmy wipes some of the pie off his shirt with his finger, smiles widely, and says, "Well, I did say that I wanted some pie, but not the whole tray!" The whole room breaks out laughing at what just happened.

Jimmy picks up the tray from the ground and walks over to me smiling. I notice that he has the clearest, most beautiful blue eyes that I have ever seen. His voice is deep. "Here, I think this tray belongs to you." He hands me the tray, and as he walks away I can feel my heart skip a beat as I lose my breath. Mrs. Betty walks up to me and whispers, "My sweet child, you be lookin' all blush after that boy be a-talkin" to ya. Everything all right?" I play off her comment quickly. "Oh, yeah, I'm okay. What boy? I didn't see any boys. Well, not any worth looking at." I wipe pie crust off of my shoulder and walk away to the kitchen. Mrs. Betty smiles.

CHAPTER 10

I wake up the next day thinking about how much fun I had volunteering at the church. I promise to myself and make a commitment to help them every week. I think about Alex for a moment and wonder when I will see him again. I think about how his treatment is going and if everything is going okay.

I get out of bed still wearing my pajamas and head downstairs for breakfast. I can hear the sound of something sizzling in the kitchen and pray that it is bacon. I walk into the kitchen just as my grandma is flipping a hot flapjack. "Hello, darlin', how would you like some hot pancakes, eggs, and maple-smoked bacon?" I lick my lips as I sit down at the table.

My grandma butters the pancakes on my plate and sets them in front of me. She places a warm cup of syrup on the table as she places another plate of bacon and eggs next to it. I pick up a piece of bacon and chomp on it loudly. "Oh, delicious, I love bacon!"

We finish breakfast just as the doorbell rings. "*Dingdong!*" My grandmother motions for me to answer it. I rush to the front door wondering who it could be this early in the morning." I open the door and see Jimmy Jensen smiling and holding a paper sack full of groceries. "Good morning, ladies, special delivery!" Jimmy looks at me and chuckles. "Smurfs are pretty cool but I prefer the Care Bears." I look down at my blue Smurf pajamas that I am still wearing and want to crawl into a hole and die from embarrassment.

Jimmy hands me the bags of food. "Thank you. My name is Pearl." I stand and stare at him as my grandmother comes from behind me and grabs the paper bags full of food. "Thanks, Jimmy. Please tell the pastor I said hello." "Will do. And hey, the church is having a musical in a couple of months if you both would like to attend." My grandmother gives Jimmy a funny face and walks back into the kitchen with the bags.

Jimmy and I stare oddly at each other for what seems like forever. I think quickly of something, anything to say to him so he will stay on our front porch. "So you like football?" I immediately feel stupid right after I say it, realizing I could have spoken about anything else other than football. Jimmy looks at me with his big blue eyes. "Football is a gift that God has given me to help others." I didn't quite understand what he meant. "Ya see, all this is so temporary. God has a higher purpose than just this. It's about helping others, the less fortunate."

Jimmy's blue eyes have captivated me, and I suddenly realize what he is talking about. I begin to think about Alex and realize that I need to somehow go and see him. Jimmy can tell that my thoughts are trailing off and intervenes. "Hey, are you and your grandma going to the church's musical show in a couple of months? I'm gonna sing a song." My head perks up in his direction. "What, is it like a talent show?" Jimmy responds quickly. "Well, yeah, it's sorta like a talent show. Anyone who would like to perform is allowed to." He places his hand on his chin. "I'm looking for someone to sing a duet with me. Do you know of anyone who can sing?" "I can!" I react too quickly to even realize what I have just gotten myself into. "Well, lemme grab my guitar and sheet music out of my car and see what you can do."

I tell Jimmy to wait a minute as I run upstairs and change. I quickly rummage through my dresser drawer looking for anything decent to wear. As I am throwing on a pair of jeans and a tank top I can hear guitar music coming from the backyard. I look out the window and see Jimmy strumming his guitar strings as he lightly starts singing a song. I think to myself how this is so different from the guys who live in my hometown. You would never see a six-foot-tall football player singing his heart out to Jesus.

I walk out to the backyard. As Jimmy sees me, he perks up. "Here, Pearl, here's the sheet music." I sit next to him as he hands me a piece of paper with the words to the song on it as he starts playing. "Okay, Pearl, let's just try the best we can since this is your first run through." I clear my throat as a huge ball of embarrassment and fear form inside of my stomach. He points at me. "Okay, go."

Whatever was inside of me was coming out and not in the musical kind of way. It was more of a chunky bacon, pancake, and egg mixture. I catch my breath as another throat full of vomit pours out of my mouth and onto Jimmy's lap. He throws his guitar to the side of him and yells, "Uugh, gross!" I finish throwing up and wipe my mouth. I look at Jimmy in embarrassment. He tries to smile, but before he can say anything I find myself running into the house and up the stairs to my room. I lock the door and promise to never come out again. I hear my grandmother pounding on my door. "Pearl, Pearl, what happened? Is everything all right?!" I stuff my head into my pillow, closing my eyes. I see the situation replaying in the back of my mind. I think about Jimmy and wonder if he will ever speak to me again. I feel my face turn red as I think about what happened over and over and over again.

I roll out of my bed and peek the corner of my eye out the window to see if he was still there. He was gone. I couldn't blame him. I just barfed up my whole breakfast on his lap. I would hate me too. I hear another knock at my door. "Leave me alone!" I yell back at it. "Pearl, Pearl, come on, let's just sing this song." Jimmy's voice rings through the wooden door. I ring back, "Aren't you mad at me? I'm too embarrassed to come out!" "Come on, Pearl, it's okay, just come out."

I open the door and look at Jimmy. He has a huge water stain over his t shirt and lap. He sticks his arms out. "So far you have spilled a whole tray of pumpkin pie slices on me and some vomit, which looked like it was some pancakes and eggs. What's gonna be next, Pearl? Come on. Please don't leave me guessing. I hate surprises!" He chuckles loudly as he hands me the sheet music again.

I find myself following him back outside. He picks up the chairs and moves them away from my vomit. "This should do." We sit back down as he starts playing his guitar again. "Okay, Pearl, you start, just sing what's on this sheet of music." I take a deep breath and start singing, my voice sounds shaky. "There will never be another who will love me like you." Jimmy smiles at me and nods his head.

"Good, Pearl, good, now sing a little louder." I dig deep into my heart and sing louder. I smile at Jimmy as he directs my voice to the sound of the music. He smiles back. Jimmy's eyebrows perk up on top of his forehead. "Good, good, sounds real nice, perfect."

We finish the song and I am actually amazed by myself. Jimmy puts the guitar pick into his mouth and claps his hands. "Bravo, bravo. Very nice, Pearl, I can't wait to perform it in front of the church!" He pats me on the back and smiles. "Hey, kids, lunch is ready if anyone is hungry!" We can hear my grandmother's voice coming toward us as she carries two plates of food to us. "Here's some turkey avocado sandwiches, I just made them." She hands them to us and then walks back into the house. Jimmy takes a bite of his sandwich and smiles. "I'm never one to pass up food!" He turns and looks at me. "So how long are you staying with your grandmother, just for the summer?" I think for a moment and realize that I can't even answer that question for myself. I try to change the subject. "So, Jimmy, how long have you lived here for?" He takes another bite of his sandwich. "All my life. Man, this football stuff wants to get heavy on your life, ya know, when I go pro. But I know God will keep me grounded."

Jimmy finishes his sandwich and I realize I have more than half of my sandwich left to eat. He gets up and I can see that his clothes have somewhat dried. "Well, Pearl, tell your grandma thanks for the food. I better get going. I gotta go and drop more food off at people's houses." He grins at me. I pick up his guitar and hand it to him. "Okay, well, I guess I'll see you later. Thanks for the song." Jimmy walks away and waves. "Let's practice once a week. How about Friday? That will give us enough time until the show." I nod my head yes, wishing that he wouldn't leave.

I see Jimmy hop into his car and peel out of the driveway. I walk into my grandmother's house and see that she's watching her soaps. I walk up the stairs and grab my Bible and start reading it. "Please, God, help me to understand all this that you have written for me."

CHAPTER 11

I sit at the bus stop waiting for the bus. I called the pregnancy center the day before and scheduled a check-up. Last night as I was reading my Bible before I went to bed, I felt a calmness and peace in my heart about keeping the baby. As my mind reminded me how hard it would be to keep it, my heart felt a connection somehow to my unborn baby. After I felt the peace overcome my heart, I got down on my knees beside my bed and prayed. "Dear God, please help me, I'm so scared, please just let everything work out." I wept for a while and then lay down on my bed to sleep. I woke up the next morning feeling somewhat reassured.

I sit down on the bus and place my hand on my belly. Another wave of doubt sweeps over me and I take my Bible out of my bag to read it. An old man sitting across from me smiles. I nod my head and look down. "All things work together for the good for those who love the Lord and are called according to His purpose." I read the scripture again and start to repeat the scripture over and over. It calms me.

I see the street that I am supposed to get off on and pull the cord, notifying the bus driver that I need to get off. He slowly stops the bus and I jump off. The road looks the same as the last time, but this time Mrs. Betty isn't dropping me off. I see the clinic in the distance and start walking toward it. My heart pounds loudly and I can feel that my feet will be swollen tonight from all the walking that I have done today. I get to the clinic and open the door.

The same receptionist is sitting at her desk, adjusting her glasses and then placing them on her forehead. "Hello, please sign in." I write my name down on the clipboard and sit down. She adjusts her glasses onto her face and reads the sign-in sheet. She looks directly at me. "Pearl, the doctor will be with you shortly." She smiles and starts filing paperwork behind her desk. I sit and wait patiently. Twenty long minutes go by and then a nurse wearing pink scrubs calls my name. "Pearl Cardello." I get up and walk to the door, following her down the long hallway. She makes me step on a scale to weigh me. "Very nice, you've gained five pounds this past month." The nurse smiles at me. I don't feel very good about what she just told me. I feel fat. I start breathing heavily as I ask the nurse questions. "How much weight will I gain throughout this pregnancy?" She looks at me and says, "Well, thirty pounds is healthy. We like around thirty pounds. Anything above that we try to intervene."

She leads me into the same check-up room and sits me down. I sit down in the chair as the nurse asks me multiple questions. Each time I answer her she scribbles notes down into my file. "Okay, Pearl, the doctor will be here to see you shortly." She hands me another paper gown and tells me to undress and put it on so the doctor can examine me. I put the gown on and sit on the exam table waiting for the doctor to arrive. Dr. Tiji opens the door and smiles. "Hello, Pearl, nice to see you again. How is everything?" I tell the doctor about my nausea and keeping the baby. "Well, that is perfectly normal, the nausea, you are pregnant." The doctor motions for me to lie down on the exam table. "Would you like to know the sex of your baby today?" I lie down on the table and tell her yes. Dr. Tiji squeezes the clear gel across my belly again and dims the lights. She places the probe on my stomach and presses firmly onto my belly.

I look at the TV monitor. The same white blob flutters across the screen. She moves the probe from side to side and says to me, "Just one moment now, I am trying to get a good picture." I lay in anticipation as the cold clear gel moves from side to side across my belly. Dr. Tiji looks into the monitor. "Well, Pearl, looks to me as if it's a boy. Ya see that right there?" She points to a piece of white blob on the corner of the monitor. "That right there is his penis." I squint my eyes and try to see what she is talking about as I question her, "Are you sure, Dr. Tiji?" She tilts her head at me and nods her head up and down. "Yes, it sure is a boy. Congratulations." She presses a small red button and a black and white picture pops out of the side. Dr. Tiji hands it to me and smiles. "Congratulations, it's a boy."

She wipes the clear gel off of my belly and places a handheld monitor on my stomach to listen to his heartbeat. Dr. Tiji nods her head. "Very nice. His heart sounds very strong." She sits me up and pages through my file. "Pearl, is there anything else I can help you with?" I shake my head and tell her no. "Everything looks great with your pregnancy. I will have the nurse give you some prenatal and iron vitamins. You should be taking them before you go to bed." She winks and smiles at me. "See you next month for another check-up." Dr. Tiji walks out of the room and I get dressed. I schedule my next appointment with the receptionist and walk out the door toward the bus stop. I stare at the picture of the baby and cry the whole way to the bus stop. I put the picture in my pocket and feel a crumpled piece of paper against my fingers. I pull it out and unfold it. It reads: "If you need someone to talk to, Dina 714-439-0617."

I stare at the piece of paper while sitting at the bus stop and debate if I should call her or not. The bus pulls around the corner and I get on. I sit in the back of the bus and pull out my cell phone and dial Dina's number. It rings twice and then she picks up. "Hello?" I clear my throat. "Uh, hi, Dina, this is Pearl." Dina's voice chirps up. "Oh, hi, Pearl. Where have you been all summer? Is everything all right?" I breathe deeply. "Oh yeah. I've been staying with my grandma. It's pretty nice out here." I try to divert the conversation quickly. "How is Trent and the weather out there?" Dina pauses for a moment and speaks softly. "Pearl, Trent and Wyoming are going out now. I thought you knew."

My heart sank into my stomach as she spoke the words into her phone. I feel my cheeks begin to burn and realize what such backstabbers Wyoming and Trent were. My voice begins to shake as I hold the phone closer to my mouth. "So Trent and Wyoming are dating?" Dina speaks conservatively. "Yeah, I was surprised also. I guess they just got back from a vacation on Wyoming's dad's yacht, somewhere in the Caribbean." I try to speak loudly, pretending that I don't care. "Well, I'm having fun at my grandmother's out here, so I better get going. Bye, Dina, thanks." I hang up the phone and look out the window. I feel betrayed and angry at Wyoming and Trent. I pull the ultrasound picture of my baby out of my pocket and stare at it again. I peer out the window and see the children's hospital in the distance. I think about Alex and pull the cord to get off the bus.

I walk down the stairs of the bus and onto the dirt road. As my feet hit the rocks I feel an excitement rushing though my veins. I can't wait to see Alex. I open the hospital door and walk down the hallway toward Alex's room. Multiple doctors and nurses rush through the hallway and into various rooms assisting each patient. I pass by the nurses' station as they are working frantically against the clock. I hear a doctor yell out. "C'mon, every minute counts. This patient isn't gonna die on my watch. She needs to get to surgery stat!" Three nurses rush down the hallway into the opposite direction and into one of the rooms.

I stand in front of Alex's door and peer into it. I feel nervous, not knowing what to expect. I see Alex lying on his bed with his eyes closed. I see a new set of stitches on the other side of his head, another fresh gauze is covering it up. I see a nurse beside his bed injecting something into his IV. I raise my finger as I motion to her. "Is it okay for me to see him right now?" The nurse finishes injecting the soluble solution into his IV and smiles at me. "Alex loves visitors. Unfortunately he just got out of surgery yesterday and has been resting a lot. He may or may not wake up, but you're more than welcome to stay and visit." She checks the monitor and walks out of the room.

I sit next to Alex's bed and look at him. He is breathing softly as he sleeps. I examine the freshly cut incisions on his head. The other side of his head looks like it has already healed. I sit and stare at Alex in his hospital bed for what seems like forever and I begin to cry. I question myself on what I can do to help Alex. I feel so sad and helpless inside. As I am weeping I hear a still small voice in my heart speak to me, "Sing, sing." I stand up beside Alex and lay my hands on his leg and weep harder. I hear the voice ring inside my spirit again, "Sing." I move my right hand up to Alex's arm and lift my left hand in the air and begin to sing. I start singing whatever song crosses my mind. "Amazing grace, how sweet the sound that saved a wretch like me."

I start weeping again, choking my words in the back of my throat as I keep singing. "I once was lost, but now I'm found, was blind but now I see." A quiet hum rings from my heart and I sing the song again. As I finish the song I sit back down next to Alex and caress his arm. I place my face next to his bed frame and begin to pray. I knew I had nothing else to offer this suffering boy but a humble open-hearted prayer. "Dear God, please heal my friend Alex. He gave me the strength to believe in you, he gave me your hope when I felt that I had nothing." I place my face in my hands and quietly cry.

"Pearl, Pearl," I hear a deep voice in the doorway of Alex's room. I look up, it's Jimmy. He walks into the room and stands next to me. It's too late to hide my tears in front of Jimmy, he already knows why I am crying. "Pearl, it's okay. Alex is a strong boy. He's gonna make it." I weep louder as Jimmy pulls me into his arms and caresses my back. "Shh, shh, everything is gonna be okay." I hold on to the back of Jimmy's sweater and shed my tears into his chest." In that moment I cried about Alex, I cried about my parents abandoning me, I cried about Chief raping me, and I mostly cried about not knowing what to expect about having a boy of my own. I couldn't help but to let it out. Unfortunately Jimmy was the only one who had hugged me in such a long time.

Jimmy held me and caressed my head as I wept. I didn't realize it but Jimmy held me for a good five minutes. After I let it all out and onto Jimmy's sweater, I push him away and realize I have put a huge wet stain on his chest. "I'm sorry about that." His big clear blue eyes look into mine. "It's okay, Pearl. I walked by the room when you were praying for him." Jimmy grabs my arm. "When are you leaving here?"

A part of me wants to jump back into Jimmy's arms as another part of me worries about telling Jimmy the truth about my pregnancy. I stand in front of Jimmy in silence and he can sense my uncertainty. "Pearl, it's okay I understand." I wonder for a moment if Jimmy knows about my pregnancy. I coax myself into thinking that he already knows about the baby. I look at Jimmy and speak. "I wanted to read Alex a story before I left." Jimmy rushes out of the room and walks back into the room holding a stack of books in his arm. I rummage through them and pick out the one that Mrs. Betty read to them a couple of weeks ago. I sit next to Alex's bed and read to him as Jimmy takes the seat at the foot of the bed. I try to do my best impression of each character in the book. I finish reading the last page of the story as Jimmy claps his hands. "Very nice. Nicely done, Pearl."

Jimmy tells me that he can give me a ride home. The whole drive home is silent. Jimmy and I both don't know what to say. Jimmy pulls up to my driveway and finally speaks. "So will you be at church tomorrow?" I answer him gently, "Of course." I open the car door and step onto the gravel road. I thank Jimmy for the ride and wave to him as he backs out of the driveway. "See you tomorrow." I walk onto the front porch of my grandmother's house and open the screen door. The sun is setting as I watch Jimmy drive his truck out and into the distance.

CHAPTER 12

My alarm goes off and I roll out of bed. Today I feel extremely tired. I have new aches and pains throughout my body, probably from the pregnancy. I open the shades on the window and let the sun shine through the glass. I stand in front of the window and stretch my body, lengthening the muscles so the soreness will go away. I take a quick shower and pick out what I am going to wear to church. I decide on a tan one-piece button-up dress. I put it on and walk into the bathroom to put some makeup on.

My skin looks dry and pale. I apply some moisturizing cream and bronzer to my cheeks so I won't look so clammy. I head downstairs and prepare myself a bowl of cereal. My grandmother usually doesn't prepare breakfast on Sundays because she is up late the night before watching her marathon soap operas. I finish my cereal and hear Mrs. Betty honking her car horn out front. I grab my Bible and run out the front door. I jump into Mrs. Betty's car. "Good mornin', child." Mrs. Betty hands me a bag of chocolate chip cookies. "I made these last night. I hope you enjoy them." She gives me a grin as she backs her car out of the driveway.

The whole way to church Mrs. Betty grins as she hums along to herself. I enjoy the quietness of the melody and feel a peace in my heart as I watch the trees pass us by in the distance. We arrive at church and sit in the front row. I see Jimmy walk in. He waves and smiles at me. I wave back. The choir walks up onto the stage and begins to sing. The whole church sings in unison. I bow my head and pray.

The pastor walks up on the stage and starts preaching to the room. "Hallelujah, glory to God in the highest!" The whole room claps and shouts out songs of praise. The pastor preaches that day about forgiveness and God's love for His people. I sit and listen as I silently pray, "God, please help this to sink into my heart." As I am praying I look up and see Jimmy out of the corner of my eye smiling at me. I nod my head at him and focus on the pastor preaching. "We must forgive others as God forgave us!" He stomps his feet onto the stage and belts out his voice into the microphone. "For God so loved the world that he gave His only begotten Son that whoever believes in Him shall not perish but have everlasting life!"

The preacher walks across the stage as random people in the audience shout out, "Hallelujah!" Claps ring throughout the room as people stand up and shout in agreement. The pastor preaches on, awakening the crowd. "We must rise up and become the church that God has called us to be, not who we think we are called to be. If God be for us, who can be against us?" The church stands in an uproar as electricity fills the room. The people all stand up and shout, "Hallelujah, glory be to God in the highest!" The preacher swiftly walks back and forth on the stage. "Forgiveness from God is for everyone. Salvation is the biggest and most important decision you will ever make in your life! Ask God for forgiveness of your sins. Whoever calls upon the name of the Lord shall be saved!"

The preacher raises his voice and snaps the ends of his words out onto the crowd. Some people from the back of the church run to the altar and get on their knees to pray and ask God for forgiveness of their sins. The choir starts singing on stage, "Change my heart, oh God." They sway back and forth to the music. "Make it ever true. Change my heart, oh God, may I be like you." Cries ring out from the floor of the altar as multiple people are on their knees weeping before the Lord. The music and the anointing of the Holy Spirit hovered in our place of prayer for the next hour. The whole church swayed to the sound of the music and sang.

As the service ends the pastor makes an announcement. "Anyone who would like to join the choir, please sign up on the clipboard in the back." As Mrs. Betty and I walk out of the service I scribble my name on the clipboard to join the choir.

Mrs. Betty drops me off at home and reminds me to take the bag of cookies with me. "Now ya all enjoy those." Mrs. Betty tilts her head. "Hey, child, I be going to a line dancin' event tonight. Would ya like to join me?" She raises her eyebrows and smiles. "I can pick you up around six o'clock if that be okay?" I think to myself for a moment and smile. "Sure." She giggles loudly and waves as I walk up the driveway and into the house.

I sit down at the kitchen table and eat the ham and cheese sandwich my grandmother had made me. I take a bite of the pickle spear and a bite of my sandwich. My grandmother calls from the living room. "So how was church, Pearl?" I shout back. "It was good." My grandmother motions a thumbs-up to me in the kitchen. "I'm going with Mrs. Betty to a line dancing event around six o'clock." My grandmother gives me another thumbs-up as she picks up the remote control and changes the channel. She giggles at a commercial that streams across the television.

I finish my sandwich and walk up the stairs to my room, examining the framed photos nailed to the wall. I see a photo of my grandmother and father when he was a small boy. They are both standing on a dock next to a lake, holding fishing poles. My father is holding a small fish in front of him. He has one of the happiest grins written across his face. I see another photograph of my grandfather and grandmother dancing on a wooden stage. They are both facing the camera and smiling. I see a photograph of my father in his graduation cap and gown. He has a gap in the front of his teeth. The picture makes me laugh. I realize how old that picture is. My father has veneers now and would never be caught dead with a gap that size in the front of his teeth.

I walk up the stairs and into my room. The cool breeze enters my room through the double-paneled windows. I take a deep breath of fresh air and lie on top of my bed. I place my hand on my belly wondering if anyone can tell that I am pregnant. I breathe deeply and start talking to my stomach. "Hey, how's it going down there? Anything new going on?" I laugh to myself.

I look at the time and decide to start getting ready. I feel an excitement in my belly. I dig in my closet and find a cherry red flannel and a pair of shorts. I put them on. I make sure that the flannel is untucked enough so you can't see my belly. I see a pair of old dusty cowgirl boots in the back corner. I take them out, brush them off, and slide them on my feet. They fit perfectly. "This will have to do," I say to myself as I start curling my hair. I place large sections of my hair into pin curls. When I am finished I grab my makeup bag and place my makeup on the bathroom counter. I put eyeliner on the top lids of my eyes and dust them with a dusty brown eye shadow. I curl my eyelashes and apply a light peachy blush to my cheeks. I grab my purse and dab lip gloss onto my lips as I walk down the stairs. I hear Mrs. Betty honking her horn. I tell my grandmother goodbye and walk out the door.

Mrs. Betty honks her horn and smiles at me as I step into the car. "My, my, my, Ms. Pearl, you be lookin' so darn cute!" Mrs. Betty giggles loudly as she pulls out of the driveway. We drive to the other side of town and pull up to a building with a large sign out front. It reads: Community Center. Mrs. Betty parks the car and we get out. As we walk to the front of the building my ears are filled with people stomping their feet, clapping, and singing along to the country music. I walk in and smile, accepting my new appreciation for country music. As we walk in an older woman in a wheelchair hands me a cow girl hat. "Here ya go, darlin'!" She winks at me as we stroll past her and sit down at a round table in the corner of the room.

The music starts blasting a famous Garth Brooks song and everybody screams and runs to the floor. A young waitress wearing a cowboy hat walks up to our table. "Hi, ladies, anything to drink?" Mrs. Betty orders us two sodas. We sip on them and smile as we enjoy watching the dance floor. The song ends and a Johnny Cash song blares over the loud speakers. Mrs. Betty nudges me and smiles. "Go on now, go and enjoy ya self." I nudge her back. "No way am I going up there. I don't even know how to line dance!" I slink back into my chair. Mrs. Betty laughs. "Oh come on now, Ms. Pearl, you can learn. It's so easy, come on!" She wiggles around in her chair and rubs her ankle. "Now you be hearin' me. My ankle be a-hurtin' real bad for a while, so you go and dance and let me live through ya." She winks at me as she nudges me out of my seat.

I slide of my chair and walk toward the dance floor. I can feel the nerves in my stomach beginning to shake. The music is playing loudly; the base makes the ground shake. I can feel the heels on my boots clicking against the wooden floor. A girl walks up to me and smiles as she grabs my arm. "Come on, it's easy." She stands me next to her and courses me in the steps to the song. We glide across the floor as we stomp our feet to the beat. I dip transversely along the floor and grab my cowgirl hat. I do a half turn as we all clap our hands and shuffle our feet. I dip to the right and then to the left and stomp twice.

As I am doing another turn across the floor I feel someone grab my arm. "Hey, you." I turn and see that it is Jimmy. He starts gliding across the floor with me as he smiles. His big bold blue eyes stand out from the crowd. "What are you doing here?" He grins and grabs my hand as we spin. "Oh, I came with Mrs. Betty." I point in her direction and can see her waving to me. The music stops and everyone shouts and claps. The music slows down and Jimmy grabs my shoulders and pulls me close to him. He looks into my eyes and starts talking. "So did you like the sermon today at church?" I stare into his deep blue eyes and shake my head yes. I feel something in my stomach and try to decide if it is pregnancy nausea or the butterflies. We sway back and forth as the music blasts throughout the room. "You're not going to vomit on me again, are you?" We both laugh in unison and I smile. "Jimmy, I'm sorry about that." "It's okay." Jimmy places his hands behind my back as he dips me. We dance across the floor, shuffling our feet to the music.

The song ends and Jimmy grabs my hand and leads me out the front door. "Where are we going?" I shout as I breathe heavily. "You'll see." Jimmy's blue eyes wink back at me as we walk through the parking lot and across the street and into an ice cream parlor. "Ice cream is like manna from heaven." Jimmy opens the door and I realize that he is still holding my hand. Jimmy shouts to the man behind the counter, "I'll have a scoop of chocolate chip mint and rocky road on a waffle cone, and whatever she wants." I look around at all the barrels filled with the creamy and colorful ice cream. I check to see if they have peanut butter and pickle ice cream and am let down when I don't see any. "I'll have peanut butter swirl and double fudge brownie on a waffle cone." Jimmy smiles at me as the man scoops the ice cream into the cone. He hands it to me and we walk out of the ice cream parlor.

We walk down the sidewalk as we eat our ice cream cones. Jimmy sets the tone for the conversation. "So, Pearl, where do you see yourself in five years?" Before I even get to speak, a young married couple holding hands walk by us. They are pushing a small baby in a stroller. The husband pulls the wife close to him as he kisses her. As I look at them my heart sinks into my stomach. I look at the baby in the stroller and ask God why did this happen to me. Why does my baby have to be the result of being raped? Why is my future ruined from one night that wasn't even my fault? I begin to think about all the horrible things that have happened to me in the past months and feel myself getting angry at God.

Jimmy nudges me. "Hey, earth to Pearl, hello?" I snap back into reality and answer him. "Well, I would like to help expand the homeless food ministry at church. The homeless have nothing, and they need to have food every day." Jimmy listens to me intently. "I would also like to help the children at the hospital. That play room is so small for them." Jimmy places his hand on my shoulder and looks into my eyes. "Pearl, you have a good heart. That's what I noticed about you." I laugh uncomfortably. "Oh, whatever, Jimmy. You have so many girls after you. You're going to go pro."

Jimmy shakes his head and looks at me. "Yeah, I go back to training camp tomorrow. It's a lot of hard work, but with God all things are possible. All those girls, Pearl." He shakes his head. "They all just see the football star Jimmy. They don't want to know the real me, like how I volunteer at the children's hospital and how I want to help people." Jimmy's voice sounds serious. "A lot of people don't even know all the hurt and pain I went through as a child." Jimmy leans into me. "I used to witness my father drinking and abusing my mother. Sometimes I would try to protect her but then he would just take it out on me." Jimmy hangs his head and looks down at his feet as we are walking. "I remember one time watching my father break my mother's jaw. I tried to help her by standing in front of her but he just picked me up and threw me across the room in a rage." Jimmy's voice begins to crack. "I remember running out of the house and to the church down the street. The doors were open. I ran into the church and fell on my knees at the altar and cried to God, pleading with him to help us. The next day my father left my mother and never came back."

Jimmy looks at the sun as it lowers on the horizon and sets in place. "That was thirteen years ago, but I had a lot of hatred for my father deep in my heart." Jimmy breathes heavy. "As time went by the Holy Spirit began to minister to my heart and reach out to me. God wanted me to forgive my father for all the hurt and pain he caused me." Jimmy looks at me. "Pearl, it was hard, but with God's mercy and grace he helped me. With God all things are possible. God made me realize that what my father did was wrong, but my unforgiveness for him was making my heart develop a root of bitterness that started to eat away at me from the inside out."

I look at Jimmy and ask him, "So how did you find it in your heart to forgive him? What if you truly hate what someone has done to you?" Jimmy turns to me. "Pearl, it took prayer and faith, believing that God would work it out for his glory. The more I was willing to let God move in me, the more he began to pour His love into me. I have to forgive because God has forgiven me. Holding on to unforgiveness and anger toward my father was only holding one person captive, me. There is a God-given freedom when you truly have it in your heart to forgive that person who has hurt you"

I begin to think about Chief and my parents again and everything that they did to me. Jimmy smiles at me. I look into his clear blue eyes. His voice has a deep huskiness to it. "I want the love and truth that God has. What he offers us is never cheap or watered down, it's real." I soon realize that we have walked to the other end of the town and are now standing under a big oak tree. The birds are chirping and the sun has already set. I look up and examine the tree as Jimmy pulls me into his arms. I wonder if he can feel my pregnant stomach and try to push him away. I want to tell Jimmy the truth. I want to tell him that I am pregnant and everything that happened, but I am too scared to. He clutches me tighter and I relax into his arms. I look into his eyes but I don't only see blue, I see a reflection of Christ in him and it attracts me to him even more.

Jimmy speaks slowly. "It's okay, Pearl, the heart that God has given you is for a purpose that he has planned for you." He leans in and I can feel Jimmy's lips on my lips as he kisses me. His upper lip is smooth and soft against mine. He slowly embraces me tighter and I can feel his heart beating against mine. I breathe deeply as he kisses me again.

CHAPTER 13

I lie in my bed the next morning and stare at the ceiling thinking about everything Jimmy and I talked about. I thought about what Jimmy was telling me about forgiveness and how anger and bitterness could be holding me captive. I get on my knees at the foot of my bed and begin to pray. "Dear God, I am very angry with Chief and my parents, I hate what they both did to me." I start weeping, as the tears are falling from my eyes I begin to speak louder. "God help me and teach me how to forgive them, I am having a hard time doing it on my own." I sit at the foot of my bed for almost thirty minutes and cry. "Help me Lord, please help me, I forgive Chief for what he did to me, and I forgive my parents." When I am done crying I feel like a burden has been lifted off of my shoulders, I feel better inside. The anxiety that I use to feel has completely vanished. I thank God and lay down in my bed. I begin to think about Jimmy and our kiss that we shared under the oak tree. I start to feel butterflies form in my belly as I smile. I think about how much I enjoy Jimmy's company and wished that he wasn't leaving. I get up and put on a pair of sweatpants and comb my hair into a ponytail. I run downstairs and sit at the kitchen table. My grandmother places a plate of warm caramel cinnamon rolls in front of me. I grab one and start eating it as my grandmother places a plate of messy eggs in front of me. I breath in the aroma of the scrambled eggs, ham, cheese and onions. I grab my fork and begin eating. My grandmother sits down and takes a sip of her coffee. "So what are you going to do today Pearl?" I shrug my shoulder and keep eating. My grandmother gets up walks to the living room and sits down on the couch. She grabs the remote and turns the television on. I hear her grumble from the living room. "Ohh, my legs feel so sore today!" She leans back deeply into the couch and relaxes. I slowly finish my breakfast and place my plate in the sink. I peer out of the window that is directly up above the kitchen sink and I can see my grandmother's garage in the near distance. "Hey, grandma what's in the garage there?" My grandmother howls back at me. "Oh, just some stuff I like to keep stored in there, you are more than welcome to look around if you would like to." I wash my dishes and wipe my hands on the dish towel. I quickly walk out the back door towards the garage. The red wooden siding on the garage looks beaten down and dirty. There are tall thick weeds surrounding the front door. The thick, tall green weeds sway with the sound of the wind as I pass by them. I stick my hand out to brush my palm against them, they feel prickly and damp. I walk up the step and open the door. It's dark and musty; I get a mouthful of rigid air and cough loudly. I look around and see a shelf in the back corner of the garage; it is filled with old outdated trinkets. I walk up to it and grab one of the dolls sitting on the self, it is covered in dust. The doll smiles back at me as I brush her of. I can feel dust fly off into every direction; I cough again and place her back onto the shelf. I see a stack of old records sitting directly underneath the shelf and on the garage floor. Those two are covered with a thick layer of filth. I crouch down and brush the top record with my hand the cover reads: "Nighttime Calypso!" Multiple colors stream across the front cover of the record. I place it back on top of the other records and move my way to the middle of the garage. I notice a very dusty cover draping over what seems to be a car. I grab one of the angles of the cover and lift it, sparks of dust fly onto my face and clothing as I sneeze in discomfort. I brush the dust off of my face and look at the car, its dark green in color and the name on the car says Chevy Impala. The car looks very old and dirty. I drape the cover back onto the car as a bike catches the corner of my eye. I grab it and wheel it out of the garage and onto the gravel road. The bike looks old, just like the car. The heavy caked on layer of dust covers the pearly white frame of the bike. I hop onto it and ride it to the house and next to the watering hose. I turn on the hose and spray all the dust off with the cool clean water. I turn off the hose and run into the house and grab a towel. I wipe off all the water from off the bike and take a step back. The white frame of the bike is gleaming in the warm summer sun; I take another step back and smile. I run into the house and throw the towel on the counter top. My grandmother is plopped in front of the television; her eyes are glued to the screen. She looks up at me for a mere second and yells, "Hey I left twenty dollars on the counter, go and do something nice today." I grab the twenty dollars and stuff it into my pocket. My grandmother winks at me. "Sorry kiddo but I have another soap opera marathon I want to watch today and I need the utmost peace and quiet surrounding me." She gives me a smile as I walk out the door and hop onto the bike.

I bike down the gravel road past Mrs. Betty's house towards town. I look at her house as I pass by; Mrs. Betty is nowhere to be seen. I ride into town wondering where I should spend the money my grandmother decided to bless me with. I pass by a bookstore with a huge red sign hanging in the window. "Fifty percent off all books." I keep riding and decide to get some ice cream where Jimmy and I started off before our big kiss. I park my bike next to the front door and lean it against the brick building. As I am walking into the ice cream parlor I can see a group of girls wearing cheerleading uniforms sitting at a table by the window. One of them looks at me and points. The whole group turns their heads to look out the window and begin to whisper amongst each other. I walk up to the counter and order two scoops of pecan praline ice cream on a waffle cone. I can see all of the girls' eyes still looking in my direction. I pay the cashier as I feel an emotion of uneasiness over come me. I walk to the back of the ice cream parlor and take a seat in one of the back booths. I try to concentrate on my ice cream until two of the girls walk up to my table. "Yup, that's her." A short blonde-haired girl points me out to her friend that is standing with her. "She's the one I saw Jimmy kissing." The other girl nudges her friend as she stares me down. "That ugly ragged thing sitting there consuming a thousand calories in one sitting?" They both look at each other and chuckle loudly; the blonde-haired girl confirms it. "Yup Jenny, that ugly thing right there was making out with Jimmy, she probably had to fool him into kissing her!" The other girl Jenny also has blonde hair and is much taller than her dim witted assistant. They both laugh again as they smooth the lining of their cheerleading skirts against their legs. Jenny fixes the ribbon in her pony tail and crosses her arms as she directly looks into my eyes. "I don't know who you think you are, but whoever you are, you better stay away from Jimmy, because he is off limits!" The two girls swiftly turn away and walk back to their table and sit down. I can feel mixed emotions of embarrassment and confusion. I finish my ice cream and walk out of the ice cream parlor. The girls eye each step I make as I walk swiftly out of the store, and hop onto my bike and ride away. I cannot phantom what just happened. "Was one of those girls Jimmy's girlfriends?" "I haven't really even told Jimmy that I am pregnant, what is he going to say?" I peddled faster trying to figure out everything that was going on. I look into the distance and can see the steeple of the church in the distance; I peddle towards it as I breathe heavily. I arrive at the church and realize that today was one of the first days for choir practice. I jump off my bike run up the stairs and walk through the double doors. A woman hands me a sheet of music and tells me to sit anywhere. I take a seat on the left side of the church. Dozens of people are eyeing the music and singing to themselves in a soft whisper. I look at the sheet music trying to memorize the words. The choir director walks up onto the stage and everybody claps. He smiles and says: "welcome everyone; we are so happy that you have decided to join the choir, glory be to God!" The choir director directs himself to the audience. "Now if you have not met me my name is Tim Jones and I am the lead choir director at this church." Mr. Jones clears his throat and keeps speaking. "Now the sheet of music that you all have been given is a song that we will be practicing for the show that the church will be putting on in a few months, we are so excited." Everyone claps and Mr. Jones directs us all to walk up on stage and stand in a line so he can strategically place us. Mr. Jones claps his hands and shouts: "Now ya'all we want the tallest ones in the back and so forth." People begin to stand back to back measuring who's taller than whom. Mr. Jones randomly points to certain people and directs them where to stand, he takes me by the hand. "Okay, now Pearl, here is your spot right here." I smile as he places me on the end of the second step on the left hand side. Mr. Jones takes about ten minutes to get us all lined up. "Okay everyone, take a look at who you are next to and tell them that Jesus loves them." Everyone turns to their right and to their left and smiles. Mr. Jones claps his hands. "Okay than let's now focus on the sheet of music that you have been given." Everyone takes out their sheet of music and places it in their hands. A small red headed woman sits down in front of the piano and begins to play the first couple of notes. Mr. Jones raises his hands to direct the choir. "Let's just sing it through and see how it feels, don't worry that it's not perfect yet." He smiles and waves his hands in the air directing us to sing. I look down at my sheet of music and begin to sing the words of the song. "He's alive whom gave us victory." "Laugh at the devil, yes you can." Some people smile and giggle as they try to make their way through the song. I can also find myself giggling at some of the lyrics of the song. Mr. Jones snaps his fingers. "Now this song is a very vibrant yet a classical song that the audience is sure to enjoy." Mr. Jones claps his hands again. "Okay now as you can see there is a small part for a solo, so if you would like to audition for that just let me know." Mr. Jones lifts his hands again and shouts: "Okay guys one more time from the top!" The whole choir starts from the beginning and sings loudly. Mr. Jones smiles widely as he directs us. Mr. Jones directs through the song a couple more times and says: "okay that's good, our practices usually last an hour, so please practice at home." The red headed woman on the piano directs us to the back of the room where they have set up trays of cookies and tea. Everyone rushes to the tables and helps themselves. I grab a large white cookie with red sprinkles on top of it and grab a cup of tea. A tall brunette woman with large cheeks comes up to me and places her hand on my back. "You must be Pearl, hello my name is Linda." She shakes my hand as she keeps talking. "I am so glad that you have decided to join the choir, I have seen you around the church a couple of times and have wanted to introduce myself." Linda smiles, gives me a big hug and walks away. "Okay see you next time, if you need anything don't be afraid to ask." I finish my cookie and tea and walk up to the table to grab another one. Mr. Jones stands in the middle of the group and speaks. "Okay, great job tonight guys, we should be getting sheet music for two more songs that I would like for us to perform." He walks away from the group and sits down and starts talking to the red headed piano player. I finish another cookie and walk down the steps of the church. When I reach the bottom of the stairs a boy a bit younger than me smiles and reaches out his hand to shake mine. "Hello, my name is Ricky and I work for the newspaper, I was given a writing assignment about our town's children's hospital." He fishes around in his pants pocket and pulls out a small recorder and holds it near his chest. "I figure it would be a great ideal to interview some of the folks spending time with the kids." He flips through a small binder and looks up at me. "I was wondering Pearl if you would do a short interview with me right now for my story." Ricky winks and smiles boldly. "Sure." I shrug my shoulders. I think to myself how there would be no harm done in a small interview. We both sit down in the pew in front of us. Ricky flips through his notes as he coughs and clears his throat. "Now Pearl, where are you from?" I look at the ground quickly as I squint my eyes as my mind is filled with thoughts of my parents." Ricky speaks again. "Pearl where are you from?" I can tell that Ricky can sense the uneasiness in my face and starts flipping through his notes again." I felt so bad inside for not answering the question, but I just had such a hard time thinking about where I was from and who I really was. In this small town I felt like a completely different person. I didn't want to tell Ricky about my dysfunctional parents and how I was raped at a party. And how somehow this small town felt almost like a security blanket. I didn't have to be the Pearl everyone knew back home who was striving so hard to be someone I didn't even know. But here I felt like a real normal person, a person I may have actually begun to like. "Now Pearl..." Ricky looks me in the eyes. "I understand if you are unable to answer some of these questions, we can think of different ones." "No, it's okay..." Ricky sits up straight and breathes deep. "Okay then, what is your favorite thing about our town's children's hospital?" I begin to think of Alex and his big smile, a smile I could never forget." I look up at Ricky and begin to speak. "I love the children there, regardless of their situation they always have so much hope in their hearts, they are always smiling no matter what." I think of Alex again and wonder what he is doing right now. "That's a great answer Pearl." Ricky scribbles notes on his paper just as quickly as he is thumbing through his paperwork with his list of questions. "Now, what have these children taught you Pearl?" I look at the ground and think of Alex and all the bandages and I.V.'s he has had to endure, I see his fragile little body sitting in his hospital bed looking out the window, smiling at the birds flying by. A tear falls from my eye as I speak. "To trust God no matter what." I wipe the tear away from my eye as Ricky pauses for a moment. He looks at me and sighs as he scripples my answer on his paper. He begins to speak again but is caught by the interruption of my voice. I look out the window to the church and breathe heavy. "I never thought I would be in a place like this." Tears begin to stream down my face. "I was a girl with so many hopes and dreams, who knows if my hopes and dreams were even a reality." "All I know is that in this moment and time I've been a fake, a phony, a fraud." Ricky quickly looks down at his tape recorder that is recording. "Ya know what Ricky??" "My name is Pearl Cardello and I am originally from a very wealthy family in California." "Not only would I shop at malls, but my mother and father owned many malls, I was so used to getting whatever I wanted, whenever I wanted, clothes, jewelry, concert tickets, you name it and I could have it," I had all the latest designer clothes and never even wore an outfit more than once. Ricky and I both look down at his worn-out tan corduroy pants as I wipe my nose. I trail on as Ricky's eyes widen. "Yes Ricky, I was that girl that everyone hated and envied, but yet I was that same girl everyone wanted to be." "I knew how they all really felt about me, I see it so clearly now." I hold my stare as I shake my head still talking. "A smile in the face and a knife in my back, who needs enemies when you have family like that." Ricky's jaw drops as more tears stream down my face. "And yes, Ricky, I did go to that party and yes Ricky I did drink, and yes a man by the name of Chief raped me, and yes Ricky I wanted an abortion so badly, I hated that man who did this to me, I hated myself and even more I hated the baby inside of me...." I place my hand on my stomach. "And here I am now hiding away in this small town." I look around the church and stare at the cross hanging from the wall across from us. "But ya know what Ricky?" By now Ricky is dumbstruck with his mouth still wide open, by now his eyes are glued to ever word I say. "Now, now I can see who I am really supposed to be..." I point to the cross. "I don't fully understand, and I don't necessarily need to know, maybe one day I will but I've learned to trust God." By now my eyes are heavily swollen from the overflow of tears. Ricky is still astonished staring at me. I stand up and begin to turn away as I place my hand on Ricky's shoulder. "These kids have taught me to have hope no matter what the circumstance may look like, that there is always a rainbow after the storm." These kids at the hospital have changed my heart and that's what matters Ricky, our heart." I turn and walk away as Ricky is flipping through his papers writing frantically as I walk out the door. At the top of the stairs I breathe deep as I see my bike and hop on it. I think about Jimmy for a moment and how much I miss him. I think about the two girls and how mean they were. Then Dina's face comes into my mind and I start feeling bad because the way I used to treat her. As I ride home I look up into the sky. "God, please forgive me for being a big bully to Dina, now I know how it feels." I tighten the grip on my handle bars. "Please heal her from any hurt or pain that I have caused her." I turn the corner quickly and petal towards the hospital. "I hope Alex is awake." My heart leaps for joy knowing that I will be with him shortly. I park my bike in the front of the hospital and make my way up to his room. Alex is on his bed looking out the window as I walk in. As he hears my footsteps entering the room he turns his head and smiles at me as he opens his arms wide for a hug. I squeeze him as tightly as I can without hurting his fragile little frame. We look into each other's eyes and smile. "Pearl!" he puts his hand up in the air for a high five, I clasp his hand and grin. I see a wheelchair next to his bed and gently pick him up. "Hey Alex, are you ready for the best adventure of your life?!" His small skinny body gently settles into the chair. "Why yes I am Pearl, oh I can't wait!" Alex begins to clap his hands and hum. I push Alex and the wheelchair into the elevator and press the button that says, "level one garden." Alex's eyes widen in excitement. "Pearl I heard that there have been so many butterflies down in the garden!" He begins to clap louder. I stare at Alex and his little body in the wheelchair as I try to hold back more tears. The elevator dings "level one." A robotic voice echoes through the hallway as I wheel Alex down the hallway and through the double doors and out to the garden. "Faster!!" Alex screams as I run down the ramp, his eyes widen with every step I take. "Wooohoooooo, oohhh yeahh!" Alex waves his arms as he giggles in excitement. I slow down as I walk through a huge arch entrance with wild flowers intertwined into it. A group of butterflies fly past us, a rainbow of colors surround us. We both breathe in excitement. We stroll down a pathway as a gentle breeze of fresh flowers fill our nostrils. I spin his wheelchair slowly in big circles as we both laugh. The sun in caressing our faces as we pass by a dozen more bushes of flowers. Alex reaches out and picks one off a stem and hands it to me. "I love you Pearl." Alex smiles, I can feel the warmth in his hand as he gives it to me. "I love you too Alex." I place the flower up to my nose and smell it. A few more butterflies glide past us, there different shapes, sizes and colors catch our eyes in amazement. "Look at that one!" Alex points to a big butterfly with wings all the colors of the rainbow." We both smile. As Alex reaches his hand out, the butterfly gently lands on him. He breathes quietly not to scare it. We both stare in amazement. Alex begins to speak softly. "One day Pearl, I'm going to be just like this butterfly." I look at him as a tear falls from my eye. "One day Pearl." Alex wiggles his finger as the butterfly gently flies away. Alex smiles and looks me in the eyes. "I'm ready to go now Pearl, I'm tired..." I turn around and push Alex past the rows of flowers and out through the arch way. Alex is breathing heavy, I can tell he is tired. We ride up the elevator in silence as Alex is softly closing his eyes. I wheel him into his room, pick him up gently and lay him onto his bed. He is already fast asleep. As I ride home I take in the cool summer breeze. I breathe deeply to calm myself so I can somewhat enjoy all the different flower fragrances as I pass by them. As my bike peddles across the dirt road I think about all the new and exciting things coming up in the near future. I place my hand on my stomach and feel a small movement pace across my belly. I stop my bike and smile as I rub my stomach. "Wow, how cool." I ride the rest of the way home smiling and enjoying my quiet time with me and my unborn son.

CHAPTER 14

I rummage through the refrigerator looking for the big jar of sweet and spicy pickles. I find it in the back of the fridge and crack it open. "*Slirrrrrrp.*" The lid pops off into my hand as the aroma of sweet pickle juice fills the room. I stick my fingers in the jar and grab a handful of the baby dills and drop them into my mouth one by one. The phone rings loudly across the living room. I skip through the kitchen eyeing my sleeping grandmother on the sofa. I pick up the phone as I clear my throat. "Hello?" "Hello, Pearl, it's Jimmy." A delicate wave of butterflies sweeps across my stomach as I smile boldly into the phone. "Oh, hi, Jimmy, how are you?" I shift my weight back and forth on both my feet as I listen to Jimmy intently. "Pearl, football camp is a lot of hard work but it's worth it. Hey, I was running laps around our field here and I couldn't get our song for the talent show outta my head. Can we practice?" Jimmy pauses as I kick my leg into the air and smile.

I look down and notice my belly and how much it is rapidly growing. I feel a sense of nervousness wanting to address the situation to Jimmy but I feel myself reluctantly holding myself back. "Sure," I reply. I immediately hear Jimmy's guitar in the background playing the beginning of our song. "Okay, Pearl, let's do it from the top." I walk into the hallway and pull the long cord of the phone with me and into the corner. I adjust my body onto the floor and cross my legs until I feel comfortable. I take a deep breath and sing into the phone. "There will never be another who will love me like you. There will never be another who can hold me, mold me." I keep singing, "There will never be another who can love me purely." Jimmy's voice gently encourages me, "Sounds great, Pearl."

We finish the song and I can hear Jimmy clapping in the background. "Good job, Pearl. I think we've got it down. I can't wait to get back to perform this song in front of the church and also see you." I feel my cheeks turning red as I say goodbye to Jimmy and hang up the phone. A smile streams across my face as I place the phone back onto the small round wooden table. "*Rinnnnnng!*" I pick up the phone quickly, expecting it to be Jimmy. "Hello, Jimmy?" The voice pauses and I can hear them breathing deeply. "Hello, Pearl, this is your father." I feel my stomach drop as my tongue goes numb. An emotion of anger quickly overwhelms me. "Hello, Pearl, your mother has informed me about what has happened and we are willing to take you back if you will just get rid of it." My father does one of his "happy chuckles" as he speaks faster. "Well, we thought it over and everyone keeps asking about you, all those questions from everyone. Pearl, we're not really sure what to tell them, and if we can just somehow make things how they were before it would make our lives a lot easier. And you know that we have a higher reputation to fulfill around here."

As his words trail off into a deeper revelation of his stupidity my mind snaps. I wasn't sure if it was my pregnancy hormones or the reality of my situation. I felt as if I wasn't one of them anymore. Not that their wealth made them any different from me, it was something more. Almost like there was something that became alive in me since they moved me out here and to my grandmother's house. "Dad, you are so selfish. All you care about is your stupid fabulous parties and your women!" I begin sobbing frantically into the phone. "The pictures, oh, all the pictures of you and those other women, cheating on Mom and me!" My voice gets higher in pitch as I try to catch my breath in between my body dry heaving. "You and Mom, for Jiminy Christmas's sake. There is more to life than just money and parties and fast cars and cheap women!"

I fall onto my knees as my stomach convulses underneath my crossed arms. "All those years growing up, I never knew you. Why did you leave me, Papa? Why did you choose all that other stuff over me?" My father clears his throat into the phone and speaks softly through the other end, "Pearl, it's not that I didn't love you. That's why your mother and I named you Pearl. Because you were one in a million." I hear him gently sigh. "Pearl, please just get rid of it and come home." I hear my father's voice grow cold as the line goes dead in my ear. I hear the dial tone and realize he hung up without even saying goodbye.

I sit down on the couch and stare at the television in my grandmother's living room and realize that her television could be older than me. I peer around the room. Everything in the living room is old, outdated, and ugly. I remember the words my father spoke to me over the phone, "Just get rid of it." I think back to my parents' house and how fabulous my life was. But now as the months had passed by something deep down inside of me didn't think that my life back home was any better than where I was now. At my parents' house I could attain anything I wanted, and here, out in the middle of nowhere, I felt as if I was finally finding out who I really was. Honestly, a part of me wanted to run back home to the plush and lavish lifestyle I had. But another part of me wanted nothing to do with it.

I put my shoes on my feet and walked through the front door. If anyone could give me any insight, I knew who could help me, Mrs. Betty. I scuffle my feet down the wooden stairs and onto the dirt road. I pick up small rocks along the way and throw them into the nearby trees swaying to the beat of the wind. I can see Mrs. Betty's house in the distance as a faint smell of Southern cooking fills my nostrils. I smile hoping that she has prepared something delicious to eat.

I walk up her front porch and knock on the door. Mrs. Betty's pearly smile beams through the window above her sink. "Ooh, child!" Mrs. Betty squeals as I hear her feet pitter patter across the floor. She opens the door and stretches her arms widely as she exclaims: "Oh, Pearl, I wasn't expectin' dinner company but come on up in here and eat something. I always be makin' some extra."

Mrs. Betty is wearing a light blue dress and a white ruffled apron. The dress skims just above her ankles as she quickly grabs my arm and paces me through her kitchen. She sits me down at the kitchen table. "Now, child, I be a-fixin' some of that good ol' fried chicken. It's my mama's recipe, now I know you be lovin' it!"

Mrs. Betty giggles as she walks to her refrigerator and pulls out a tall jar of cold and sweet iced tea. She pours me a glass and places it in front of me. "Now, Ms. Pearl, what do I owe the honor of you be arrivin' here so up and suddenly?" Mrs. Betty winks in my direction as she walks to her frying pan. She dips two large pieces of chicken into a yellow thick batter sitting on the counter. She plops them into the frying pan. They sizzle loudly as Mrs. Betty begins to chuckle loudly. "Oh, Ms. Pearl, this be my mama's secret fresh fried chicken recipe. I be makin' this sometimes once a week!"

Mrs. Betty grabs a glass of sweet tea that's sitting next to the oven. "Oh, it be gettin' hot up in here fryin' all these chicken pieces, but oh, child, it be worth it!" She grabs a large wooden spoon and stirs a bubbling pot on the other corner of the stove. "Ms. Pearl, I hope you be likin' green beans and bacon. I also made some mashed potatoes, gravy, and some homemade cornbread."

I congratulate myself in the back of my mind as I realize this was the perfect time to show up to Mrs. Betty's house. The aroma in the kitchen makes my stomach grumble loudly. Mrs. Betty walks over to me and places the palm of her hand on top of my belly. "Oh sweet baby from heaven, this baby is gonna love some of this fried chicken, uh-huh!"

I place my hand on top of my stomach and look down to the ground. Mrs. Betty runs to her oven and props it open. The smell of sweet cornbread overwhelms me as I begin talking. "Did you ever want to abort your son?" I feel bad asking her the question but I needed some answers. Mrs. Betty walks to the other end of the wooden table and sits down across from me. "Honestly, child, yes, I did. I was so hurt from what that man did to me and how everything was turning out that I began to hate that small baby that was inside of me. I remember many nights crying in hopelessness."

Mrs. Betty places her hand, which is covered in chicken coating, on her hip. She begins to shake her head and stares straight into my eyes and says, "I remember the night it happened. Some of my girlfriend's and I lied to our parents and told them we would be at the movies. Instead, we went to hang out with some of the 'bad' boys who went to our school. Oh, child..." Mrs. Betty begins to breath heavy and tilts her head. "The whole town's adult folks would always say how much of a bad character those boys be carryin', but sometimes, Pearl, we only want to see what we want to see."

I look at Mrs. Betty's face and she is half dazed as if she is somewhat replaying a memory to herself. Mrs. Betty grabs a few pieces of fried chicken from the frying pan and places them on a plate on the counter with a few of the other pieces. She quickly dips a few more pieces of raw chicken into the batter of hot oil. As she drops it in I hear it sizzle loudly. Mrs. Betty places the fork on the counter and gracefully strolls across the kitchen and sits into the chair across from me. As she sits she grabs a napkin on the table and blots the sweat on her forehead. "Oh, child, that's much better."

She smiles at me and begins speaking again. "The night it all happened, these boys were so, so charming at first…" Mrs. Betty's gaze looks down at the table. "Me and my friends were actually having a good time. The boys stole some alcohol from one of their dads and everyone was drinking. Now, Ms. Pearl, I ain't never drank before, but with all of my friends and the boys tellin' us everything would be fine, I just figured it be best for me to be just fittin' in. One of the boys, Tommy, kept giving me more alcohol, Ms. Pearl. I ain't never drank before. Well, it wasn't before a matter of time that I started to feel really sick, so that boy named Tommy thought it be a good idea to take a walk by the river. We sat and chatted the best I could. He was so kind and sweet until he tried to kiss me. I pushed him away, and oh, Pearl, that young boy became enraged."

Mrs. Betty's eyes began to widen as she kept speaking. "I kindly tried pushing him away again, and the next thing I knew he pinned my arms to the dirt ground and was on top of me." Ms. Betty's eyes widened and she was now grasping her hands together on top of the table. "Oh, child, I was so scared. I wanted to scream but he had his hand over my mouth."

All of a sudden we are interrupted by the hallway fire monitor beeping loudly. Ms. Betty jumps up and runs over to fan some air into it. "Ms. Pearl, take that chicken out of that heavy grease before it be lightin' this whole house up."

I jump up and run across the room. The smell of fried chicken fills my nostrils even more. I plop the few pieces onto the plate as Ms. Betty smiles at me. "See, child, you're going to be a great something of a mother and wife someday for someone very special."

I sit back down in my chair as Ms. Betty meticulously places more of the chicken into the frying pan. She lifts the lid to the bacon green beans and stirs them. As her back is still turned away from me I listen to her speak. "Ya know, Ms. Pearl, that boy Tommy got off for what he did to me." Ms. Betty gazes out of the window. "I was somewhat blamed for my behavior, for lying to my folks, and even worse, nobody saw what happened. Tommy's lawyer argued that I was something of a loose girl who went to bed with Tommy and was trying to get something of revenge because he dumped me." Ms. Betty's gaze was glued to the trees swaying in the wind outside her kitchen window. "And they all believed him. I was the only one who knew."

Ms. Betty looked down at the frying pan and quickly flipped the chicken and sighed. "Oh, Ms. Pearl, all that hatred and anger in my heart from that one night." Ms. Betty went on. "I was devastated. My parents were devastated and so ashamed of what had happened, and they almost made our family leave town. See, Ms. Pearl, back in those days people talked a whole lot. Everyone had somethin' of an opinion and somethin' to say." Ms. Betty looked down at the pan. The hot oil and chicken cracked and sizzled as a tiny flame overcame the bottom of the pan.

There was a long silence of what seemed to be forever, and then Ms. Betty spoke. "Ms. Pearl, I was of that young girl age, the age of gettin' a period. We didn't know much about the birds and the bees, but after I missed my period a few months in I knew somethin' was going on. Ms. Pearl, me and my momma done found out that I be carrying a child from all that happened."

I look at Ms. Betty's face and see a tear fall from her eye. She places her hand on her heart and begins to weep. "Ms. Pearl, I was so young. I didn't know nothin' about nothin'. I never had no man, not even a boyfriend. And now I be what they sayin' 'with child.'" Ms. Betty breathes deep and refocuses her eyes on the chicken. "I didn't know what to do. I was so ashamed and scared… And all those people in town, oh, the horrible things they be talkin' about me and my family."

Ms. Betty rearranges the chicken in the frying pan and sighs heavily. "I didn't want nothing to do with nobody after all that. I began to isolate myself from the world and deny that I was even with child." Another tear falls from her eye as she speaks even softer. "I wanted nothin' about nothin' to do with that baby. Every day I had so much hate and anger about what happened, about how it was my fault, how I could have avoided it all. I had so much hate and anger inside of my heart for that boy that did that to me and also for that baby that be a-growin' inside my belly."

Ms. Betty begins to fix me a plate of food. As she places a rather large piece of cornbread upon my plate I feel my stomach grumble. She places the full plate of fried chicken, green beans, mashed potatoes, and cornbread before me. My eyes widen in amazement as I grin.

Ms. Betty sits next to me and grabs my hand as she closes her eyes. I can see the wet traces of tears that have already streamed down her face. Her voice this time is filled with a calm confidence as she speaks. "Ms. Pearl, every day since that night I be wantin' to do nothin' but just get rid of that baby. I be hatin' every day of my life. One day while walking through my grandma's house I came across a Bible just there sittin' on her dresser. I wanted nothing to do with that religious stuff. I mean my mama always would bring us to church but nothin' neva clicked with me." Ms. Betty's eyes are still closed as she is also still holding my hand while speaking. "Ms. Pearl, I swear it must have been nothin' but the Lord Almighty reachin' straight out to me in that moment of time."

Her eyes are still closed as she starts shaking my hand this time while speaking. "Ms. Pearl, I done opened that Bible right there and it's almost as if God Himself spoke to me. 'For God so loved the world that He gave His only begotten Son, that whosoever believeth in Him should not perish, but have everlasting life.'" Another tear streams down her face as she keeps talking. "Ms. Pearl, in that moment, I didn't barely know what all that really meant, but it's almost as if I felt the good Lord Himself touch my heart in that moment way back then. In that moment I felt the hand of God on my heart. I felt His unconditional love for me, and I also felt His love for that baby in my tummy."

Another tear streams down Ms. Betty's eye. "I knew then that God was gonna help me. I knew it wasn't always gonna be easy, but somehow, Ms. Pearl, I knew deep down inside that God was gonna always be there for me and that there baby." Ms. Betty then looks me in the eye as she tilts her head. "Ms. Pearl, I'm so sorry for some of the things your heart there has been feelin'. I do see the pain in your eyes and the Lord has been havin' me pray for you every day. I know you may have a lot of questions, but, Ms. Pearl…" Ms. Betty directs her eyes up and points to the sky. "Ask Him."

She then gives me a smile of reassurance as she rubs my back and gets up from the table. I can hear the sound of pots and pans clinking in the background as Ms. Betty walks back and forth from her stovetop to the counter. I begin to feel the warmth of the tears fall down my face; this time I am unable to stop them. They are heavy and warm as they drop down onto the table. I cover my hands with my face trying to somehow stop them. "Why, God, why?" I can feel a pit in my stomach as the tears flow even more. "God, I don't understand. Please help me. Please help me, God." A few more whimpers come out as the aroma of food from my plate fill my nostrils. I pick up my napkin and wipe away any tears that were still on my face. I take a deep breath, sigh, and begin to eat my food.

CHAPTER 15

"Just get rid of it, just get rid of it, just get rid of it…" *Beep, beep, beep!* I am half awake and shaken from the sound of my alarm clock going off and my father's voice echoing in the back of my mind. I look down. My pink fluffy pajamas are tight around my belly and I can see that I am showing. I put my hand on my belly and somewhat grin. My head is still a little unsure, but my heart feels as though I'm all in for the tough journey ahead of me.

I kick my legs off of the bed and walk across the room to my dresser. I open it and begin to get dressed. Today is the church's talent show and Jimmy is still stuck at football camp. I am somewhat happy that Jimmy is still gone, realizing that it has bought me more time to avoid explaining my situation to him. I decide on a light blue one-piece dress. It hugs my belly and definitely shows everyone that indeed I am pregnant. I choose tan boots, tie my hair in a quick ponytail, and add a few strokes of mascara. I'm way too tired to get all dolled up for this event. If I can make it through today without falling asleep in front of anyone it will be a true miracle.

I hear Ms. Betty's car pull into the driveway and her honking. I glide down the stairs and grab a granola bar and banana and am out the door. I see Ms. Betty's wide smile as I plop myself into her car. "Well, good ol' mornin', Ms. Pearl." I smile at her as I buckle my seatbelt. Ms. Betty doesn't say much but hums the whole way to church. We pull up into the church parking lot and Ms. Betty helps me wedge my body out of the car. I can feel the heaviness of the baby in my stomach and feel like I am somewhat waddling as we walk in through the church doors.

The place is already packed with the more than usual crowd. People scatter all through the sanctuary shaking hands with one another while they introduce themselves. I take a seat in the last back pew and try to somewhat place my feet up. I look down at my belly and can see how much it has grown these past months. I then feel a kick inside my belly and place my hand on my stomach with excitement. "Hey there, baby." I rub my belly and close my eyes to rest them; all seems well in that moment in time.

I am awoken by our choir director clapping his hands and telling everyone to get up on stage and take their places. I waddle my way up to the second row on the left-hand side. I stand in my place and feel as if my belly is rubbing up against the girl's head in front of me. She has a big poufy ponytail that every time she moves tickles my belly button. I try not to laugh as our choir director is eyeing each one of us and reminding us about our posture.

Everyone stands up straight as the piano player and drummer begins to play. All of our voices chime in to the beat of the drums as we all begin to clap in unison. A slow and steady sway overtakes each row as the audience follows by clapping along with us. Our choir director smiles. We can all tell that he is well pleased with our performance so far. We finish the first song as the audience claps and the music slows down to a steady pace. I move from my spot and walk to the front and center of the stage and grab the microphone. The choir director asked me last week on short notice to fill in for a solo performance because one of the girls, Katie, had gotten sick with the flu. I agreed, but now, looking at the vast majority of the packed sanctuary, I wished I hadn't.

The room was dark and the lights were dim. I held the microphone up to my mouth and began to sing. Smiles swept across the room as my voice began as somewhat shaky and then I smoothly and slowly sing the word to each note. I scan the room with my eyes and see Ms. Betty in the audience smiling at me. I relax my nerves and really start getting into the song, even snapping my fingers while I sway back and forth. The choir behind me jumps in quickly and sings loudly for their part. I smile as my eyes gaze back and forth across the room.

I look to the back corner of the room and see Jimmy looking right at me. My heart begins to race and I feel my face getting hot. His eyes are directly on me and my pregnant stomach. My voice somewhat cracks as I try to concentrate on the tempo of the music and what words of the song I may have missed. In that moment I'm not sure what to think. All I know is that I wanted to jump off the stage and run to Jimmy. I wanted to somehow explain myself and for him to just hold me and tell me that it's all going to be okay.

I finish singing the last chorus as the audience applauds. I put the microphone back and walk off the stage and run toward the bathroom right past Jimmy with my face down. "Pearl, Pearl!" I run out of the room as Jimmy chases after me. "Pearl, wait. Stop!" I stop in the middle of the hallway, only for us to see a small group of children playing "duck, duck, gray duck" with their teacher. They all stop and look at us.

"Jimmy, what are you doing here? I just can't face you right now." Tears flow down my face. I soon realize the children and their teacher all have their eyes fixated on me talking. "Jimmy, I'm so sorry. I never wanted to lie to you, but I was so scared to tell you everything and how I just hated my life and my situation. But God has shown my heart a different way to live." Jimmy looks into my eyes. I turn my body to walk away. "I'm sorry, Jimmy, I just can't do this right now." Jimmy grabs my hand. "Wait, Pearl."

Now the teacher and children fixate their eyes on Jimmy. He then takes a folded-up newspaper from the back of his pocket and puts it in front of my face. It was the interview I did months ago after choir practice with Ricky. I look at it in disbelief. "Ya see this, Pearl, this is the girl I fell in love with months ago. You didn't tell me but I knew, and I knew how scared you were and maybe are, but I know how God can take situations like this and use them for His glory." He places my hand in his hand and kisses it. "Pearl, it's always been you. I know I may only seem like a small-town football guy but I know God, and I also know once I get drafted into the NFL God will take care of us." Jimmy then places his hand on my belly as he gazes into my eyes.

"Aw!" We look over at the voices. We had forgotten that we were being watched this whole time by a teacher and her five-year-old students. Jimmy then pulls me close as all the kids begin to chant, "Kiss her, kiss her!" Jimmy pulls me close and gently lays his lips upon mine. "Ew," the kids screech as they all begin to jump, clap, and laugh. "It's going to be okay, Pearl, I promise." I feel my heart beat fast as Jimmy pulls me closer and holds me. "There's no place I would rather be than here."

I close my eyes and rest my head on Jimmy's shoulder as he strokes my hair. Just then the pastor walks by. "Hello, brother Jimmy!" He gives Jimmy a big hug. "We didn't know you were going to be here, I heard that the choir director had to cancel your and Pearl's performance." Jimmy looks down. "Yes, Pastor, I'm sorry about that. I thought I was still going to be stuck at football camp." The pastor smiles, "Well, Jimmy, I'm sure I could put in a word if you two still wanted to perform." Jimmy looks at the pastor, then me, and smiles.

Jimmy and I are now on stage, and back behind the curtain the choir director looks at us as he motions for us to come onto the stage. Jimmy grabs my hand and helps me onto one of the stools sitting in the middle of the stage. He sits on the other stool and places his guitar on his knee. He looks at me and nods as he begins to play. The strings of the guitar strum throughout the sanctuary; I can tell he's been practicing. "There will never be another who will love me like you; there will never be another who could hold me, mold me. There will never be another who could love me purely... No there will never be another who has loved me like you."

Jimmy grins and nods at me to start my part of the song. I close my eyes and sing. And in that moment I see my past life. I see my mother and father. I see Zelda baking her famous blueberry muffins, and I see my old friends from school, and my heart somewhat breaks for them. I sway back and forth to the music as Jimmy and I both sing our parts into our own separate microphones. I see Ms. Betty in the audience. We lock eye contact for a mere moment and she nods her head graciously. We finish our song and the audience claps loudly. Jimmy grabs my hand to stand and take a quick bow. The audience stands to their feet in an uproar of applause. Jimmy looks at me and winks. I squeeze his hand and smile.

CHAPTER 16

Ms. Betty and I are on our way to the children's hospital. Ms. Betty is doing her classic humming away while driving the car. I look at the stack of books on my lap and stuffed animal I got for Alex. My heart leaps in excitement knowing I will soon see him. I peer out the window as Ms. Betty weaves in and out of traffic. I've noticed that the tree leaves have changed colors and the tree branches are somewhat bare. I try to hum along to Ms. Betty's tune as I relax into my seat in the car. We pull up to the hospital. Ms. Betty finds a parking spot near the front and pulls in. "Oh, thank you, sweet baby Jesus." She turns and smiles at me. "Oh the good Lord knew my feet were a-hurtin' today!" She gives me a giggle, only to lift her foot and show me that she is wearing her hot pink fuzzy house slippers. I laugh as I open the car door.

Ms. Betty is still giggling loudly as she slams her car door and locks it. "Oh, Ms. Pearl, my dawgs be a-barkin' since last night." I follow closely behind Ms. Betty, only to notice the fuzzy top part of her house slippers blowing in the wind. I smile again as we enter the hospital. We get into the elevator and Ms. Betty picks the floor number. The elevator dings as the doors open to our floor. As soon as we step out we hear a loud ding echoing throughout the hallway. "Code red!" A doctor and group of nurses run past us quickly. "What room is it?" the doctor yells to one of the nurses. "Room 314!" A male nurse soon rushes past us with a machine on wheels.

Ms. Betty looks me in the eyes. "That's Alex's room." My heart drops as I run to follow the group of doctors and nurses rushing to Alex's room. I run through the door, only to have a nurse push me out of the room. "That's my friend Alex! Please let me see him!" The nurse firmly holds my arms as she removes me farther from his room. I can see Alex's little feet on the bed. I can see doctors and nurses working frantically on him. One doctor is performing CPR on him while another is sticking IVs in his arm. All I can hear is a heart monitor going off and a doctor firmly yelling at his staff. I start crying uncontrollably, begging the nurse to let me in. "Please, please!" I yell in between each tear that falls down my face. The nurse looks me in the eye. "Ma'am, please, let us help him. Wait here. I will come back." The nurse then runs back into the room to help.

"Code red, code red!" The alarm is still ringing throughout the hospital hallway. Ms. Betty comes from behind me and embraces me. "Will Alex be all right?!" Ms. Betty caresses my hair while I weep. "Please, God... Please, God, let Alex be okay..."

Ms. Betty and I make our way to one of the waiting rooms down the hallway. We sit and wait for what seems like forever. A few hours go by and as I begin to drift off to sleep with my head cradled by my hand Ms. Betty jumps up and walks to the door. "Dr. Pierre!"

The doctor turns to her as she speaks quietly with him in the hallway. As they are both talking I see Ms. Betty looking at me with candid yet sorrowful eyes. The doctor shakes his head and walks away. Ms. Betty looks at me as she sits down and places her hands on my shoulders. "Now, Ms. Pearl, you need to know that they did everything they could do. I'm sorry but Alex is gone." In the moment I feel as if someone just kicked me in my stomach. "No!" I scream loudly as Ms. Betty tries to pull me close to her. "No, God, please not Alex!"

I break free from Ms. Betty's grip and run down the hallway to Alex's room. Deep in my heart I wished for him to be there. I thought of every time I came and visited him and his big smile that would just light up the room. I ran faster through the hospital hallway and into his room. Alex's room was quiet and dimly lit by a Superman nightlight next to his bed. I close my eyes and breathe heavy, not sure whether to take the step into his room or run away. I sit on his bed and begin to weep. I grab onto Alex's pillow as if it were him and cry deeply. I feel such sorrow in my heart as I cry for what seems like forever.

I look up on the walls next to Alex's bed and see what seem to be pictures Alex had drawn. I begin to weep harder seeing that one of the pictures he drew had three people in it. The black crayon traced onto the page a wheelchair with Alex sitting in it smiling. Underneath the wheelchair was scribbled his name, "Alex." I notice a somewhat stick figure pushing the wheelchair, the figure has a bright colorful dress filled in with flowers. Underneath the figure is the name written, "Pearl." I see Alex also drew a small baby figure where my stomach is supposed to be, labeled "Baby." The baby has a huge red heart above him and is smiling.

I weep even harder as I pull the picture off the wall and hold it. My tears drip onto the page and soak into the paper. I see in the upper right-hand corner Alex drew a bright yellow sun shining with a huge smiley face. All the clouds, trees, and plants are also accompanied with smiles. "Why, God, why would you do this to him? He was so fragile and had a heart of gold!" I scream at the ceiling as if God was right in front of me. I turn the piece of paper over and see that there was a note handwritten by Alex. It reads:

> Dear God, I thank you for my friend Pearl! She is so nice and pretty! I enjoy the times she pushes me in my wheelchair outside by the garden. I know she is going to have a baby, God, and maybe she might be scared like how I am scared when I go in for surgery. But, God can you please help her like how you have helped me so many times? And also, if she doesn't know you, I hope she will know you so I can see her again in heaven.

> Alex

> Oh, and PS, if it's not too much maybe you could ask Pearl to name her baby after me.

The end of the note had a huge smiley face at the bottom. I cry even harder in my moment of grief. I feel as if the loss of Alex is too much to handle. Ms. Betty walks into the door and sees the picture I am holding in my hand. She rubs my back and says, "Ya know, Ms.

Pearl, Alex really loved you. And you need to know that while he was here on earth you made a difference in his life. And also, Ms. Pearl, you need to know that Alex made a difference in your life too." I look down at my stomach and realize Alex was one of the reasons I chose to keep my baby. I didn't know it then but in that moment I realized that in the short time Alex was here he impacted my life and showed me what unconditional love and kindness really are. "Thank you, God, for letting me know him. Please help me to deal with this grief. My heart feels so heavy."

Ms. Betty and I both sit in Alex's empty, silent room and cry.

CHAPTER 17

"PUSH! PUSH!" My legs are in the stirrups at the hospital as sweat drips down my face. My water had broken in the middle of the night. I called Ms. Betty and she drove me straight to the hospital. I hadn't dilated for the past seven hours and now the doctor was telling me it was time to push.

The doctor looks me in the eyes as I scream in pain. "Now, Pearl, I need you to breathe deep and keep pushing." I take a deep breath and push harder than before. A sharp pain comes out of me as I scream even louder than before. And then I hear it. The first cry of my baby. Everyone in the room works fast to place him on my chest and wipe him clean. Baby whimpers, an almost catlike sound that fills the room. I hold him close to me so he can feel my warmth. As he places his tiny hand on my face a tear streams down my cheek. I look at his beautiful face and cannot believe what I had just gone through in the past few hours. The same hospital that Alex had passed away in, I am only a few floors below giving birth to life.

The nurses grab the baby. "Pearl, we need to cut the umbilical cord." I look over and see the doctor make one swift movement across his small belly. The nurse then wraps the baby tightly in a light blue blanket, places a tiny light blue hat on his head, and lays him back on top of my chest. He feels warm against my skin and I realize there was nowhere I would rather be but in this moment. She smiles at me. "Congratulations! What is his name?" I place my finger on his tiny nose that looks exactly like mine. "Alex. His name is Alex…"

A note from the author:

I hope you enjoyed reading the book *Broken Pearl*. My prayer for you while writing this book was that you would experience God's unconditional love for you and that He would reveal Himself to your heart in a tangible and mighty way. We all make mistakes in our life, but you need to know that God's love will never fail for you. If you have never received Jesus in your heart and would like to right now, you can pray this simple prayer to make Jesus Christ your Lord and Savior. It's not so much how you pray the prayer but that you simply open your heart to receive it.

> Dear Lord Jesus, I know I am a sinner and that you died and shed your blood on the cross for all my sins to be forgiven. Please forgive me for all of my sins. Today I receive you in my heart and in my life. I thank you that by receiving you in my heart today the Bible says that old things have passed away and all things have become new in Christ. Today I receive your forgiveness, love, healing, and wholeness in Jesus's name. I thank you that today is a new day in Jesus's name, Amen.

If you prayed that prayer we believe that you are born again. Get into a good Bible based church and believe God that your life will never be the same.

ABOUT THE AUTHOR

Faith started writing in high school for her local newspaper, *The Star Tribune*, at the mere young age of seventeen. Faith knew God had given her a passion to write. Years later, while a pregnant single mother living in poverty, Faith still had a desire to write. She picked up a job at a local newspaper. She wrote and had multiple articles published in the *Westminster Herald*, a newspaper located in Westminster, California. After her first son Malachi was born she felt the Lord begin to stir in her heart the story of *Broken Pearl*. The book written solely by the guidance and direction of the Holy Spirit was written in her parents' basement within a week. Uncertainty and insecurity kept the story *Broken Pearl* sitting on Faith's laptop for seven years. After overcoming three years of severe health issues, Faith felt again the Lord speak to heart to finish *Broken Pearl*. With the help and encouragement of her local church, friends and family *Broken Pearl* was finally completed. *Broken Pearl* is a story near and dear to Faith's heart. Faith is currently divorced and lives in Irvine, California, with her two sons—Malachi, aged eight; and Caleb, aged five. She enjoys writing, hiking, traveling, and eating out.

Faith also has a passion of creating awareness for the importance of mental health and reducing the stigma associated with it. She is committed to starting her own ministry, a vision that the Lord has put on her heart called Mental Health Matters, after going through and experiencing her own struggles of mental health issues after both her children were born. Faith is dedicated to spreading awareness and hope to those going through similar situations. "Mental health is nothing to be ashamed of, we all will experience it in one way or another, whether it be ourselves or someone we care for and love."

CPSIA information can be obtained
at www.ICGtesting.com
Printed in the USA
LVHW040741171120
671899LV00019B/414/J

9 781098 050580